A Child's Journey through Foster Care
by Carole Klock

Acknowledgments

I would like to thank and express appreciation to a few special people who have helped me in writing this story.

My husband, Harry, has supported me throughout the long process of telling my story. There have been times, I am sure, that his patience has been stretched to the limit. He is my best friend and confidant. Thank you, Harry, for believing in me.

Lee Warren, my editor and friend, has been phenomenal. From the time I met him several years ago at a writer's conference, he has become a mentor to this rank beginner. By the time several writers' conferences had come and gone, and I needed an editor for my book, there was only one choice for me. He has been a friend, an encourager, and a teacher. Thank you, Lee, for your time, patience; and especially your friendship.

For the ladies in my writing group, thank you for all your editing, critiques, and especially your love and encouragement. You are all special blessings.

A special thank you to Brian Ward, my friend and fellow church member. Your suggestions and encouragement have been a real blessing. Thanks for all the e-mails and proofreading. I appreciate you very much.

To my foster brother, Ed. It has been a long, long road for us both. I am so thankful that you are my big brother. Thanks for your love and support.

Finally, I give praise and thanks to my Lord and Savior, Jesus Christ. He promised when I was just a small child that He would turn my upside-down life right side up. That promise has been fulfilled and He has given me back the years the locusts had eaten. He walked beside me every step of this long journey. Thank you, Lord Jesus.

Introduction

My mother quit high school to marry my father. She had no education or special training. The only jobs she could find were low paying entry level positions.

When I was old enough to understand, Mother tried to explain the situation to me. My parents were very young when they married. The marriage lasted six years. Mother said the first three years were wonderful and the last three were terrible. My dad was not faithful, and he was a gambler. I don't remember him. I was just two years old when he walked away. I never saw him again.

When Mother found herself alone with two children in a post-depression economy, she simply did the best she could for as long as she could. No one in her family volunteered to help and she received nothing from my father or his family. Money was really tight. Mother said, "When it came to the point that you and your brother, Billy, had one good pair of shoes between you and were thin and pitiful looking, I had to admit I needed help."

She explained that AFDC (Aid to Families with Dependent Children) didn't exist at the time and there were no welfare programs. The only option available was to place her children in foster care. Very reluctantly, she made an appointment with The Children's Aid Society of Pennsylvania.

She spent most of that day being interviewed, filling out papers and making the arrangements for my brother and me to be placed in foster care. After she completed the paperwork, the social worker—a kind woman—urged my mother to take the weekend to think everything through. "Spend some time with the children and you can come back Monday to sign everything," she said. Mother went back; nine months later.

Chapter 1
Not a Bad Girl

My first year in foster care, I lived in five different foster homes. Only two of them left any lasting memories. One was a happy place with several children in the family and several foster kids. The house was new. Winter had set in and the lawn would not be planted until spring. Wide boards were stretched across the dirt to provide a walkway up to the front door and also out to the backyard. I remember a lot of laughter and fun. We children spent much time chasing each other through the house and out to the muddy yard. I was happy there. Even though my memory of those times is dim, I do remember being moved suddenly to a new home. No one bothered to explain to me why.

Years later, I learned from my mother that my foster mother at that home had become ill and had to give up her foster kids. Eventually, even her children had to be taken in by family members.

The only other home I remember was different. I was the only child in the home. I am not certain how long I stayed there, but I know it was not long. It could have been only a matter of weeks or at the very most, a couple of months. My foster mother at that home seemed very nice and treated me well, never abusing me. However, she sent me back to the agency, saying, "She's absolutely incorrigible." I had no idea what incorrigible meant, but I got the message very clearly. I was bad.

Let me tell you how bad I was. Shortly after coming to this home, I was outside playing in the back alley when I ran into my big brother. I mean we literally collided. He was riding his bicycle and wearing his goofy leather pilot's cap with the ear flaps and goggles. I recognized that cap right away. Billy loved that cap and wore it all the time.

"Billy, is that you?" I was overjoyed to have found him.

"Yeah, it's me. What are you doing here?"

"I live here now," I said.

"I live just around the corner," he replied. "Come on, I'll show you."

It was an easy walk from my house to his. We could play together. I could be with my big brother again! I felt like I'd been given a special gift, just to be near him after being separated for so long. He was my friend, my hero, and my only connection to my real family. From then on, the minute I was allowed to go outside to play, I headed straight to his house.

My joy was short lived. My foster mother came looking for me. When she found me, she was really upset and gave me a good scolding.

"This is too far for you to come to play." She marched me right home. "It is not safe for you to go that far."

My little brain was screaming, "How could it not be safe? I'm with my big brother!"

She repeated herself, "You cannot go that far by yourself."

"I wasn't by myself! I was with my big brother!"

She restricted me to the house for the rest of the day.

Why am I being punished? I just want to be with my brother.

The next day when I was going out to play, my foster mother asked, "Now, will you be a good girl?"

As I told her, "Yes," I thought, *Of course I'll be good; I never meant to be bad!*

As soon as I was outside, I ran my little legs right to my brother's house. Again, my foster mother came looking for me. Again, she made me stay in the house for the rest of the day. She made me promise when I went outside the next day that I would be good.

This little drama repeated itself over and over. I could not understand why my foster mother insisted it was not safe for me. It wasn't that far! I knew Billy would keep me safe.

My foster mother threatened to send me back to the agency if I didn't obey. I simply didn't believe her. Mothers, even if they were only foster mothers, just didn't send their kids away. Then, one awful day, I overheard her talking on the phone. She was speaking to someone at the agency. "You will just have to send someone to come and get her because she will not obey." I was stunned.

I could hear my own voice in my head, shouting, *How can adults be so stupid? Why can't my foster mother see that I have to be with my big brother? Why doesn't she understand? Billy won't let anything happen to me. He is four years older than me and he will take care of me. Don't tell the social worker that I am bad! It's not true! I'm not bad! Billy will protect me and make sure I get home safely. Don't you know that Billy took care of me when my mommy worked nights and had to sleep during the day? Don't you know he propped a kitchen chair under the doorknob to our apartment? He's my hero. He's the only connection I have to my family? What do you mean I'm not allowed to go play with him? What is the matter with you adults? Don't you understand anything?*

The agency sent a social worker to the house and I was moved again. I have a clear memory of standing in the living room between my foster mother and the social worker, listening to an account of how bad I was. They were talking about me as if I weren't even in the room.

"She just will not obey," my foster mother told the social worker.

"We will have to place her in another home," the social worker said.

No one cared what I thought or how I felt. From that time on, I dreaded visits from social workers. They were mean, and I refused to trust any of them.

I was moved to a new home in the suburbs of Philadelphia, far away from my big brother. My little heart was broken. I believed that I was being punished for no other reason than wanting to be with my brother. The adults who controlled my life were going to make sure I would not be able to see him again. I was four years old, and I already knew despair.

YEARS LATER, MY BROTHER, Bill, took me back to that old neighborhood. He'd dropped the "y" and preferred to be called just Bill. I was a young mother with two small children. My husband, Harry, was deployed with the Marines. I drove over to New Jersey where Bill lived with his family. It was a special treat for us to spend the day together. On this particular day, it was just Bill, myself, and my two little ones, Tommy and Linda. Out of the blue, Bill said, "Come on, let's go for a ride." He didn't tell me where we were going; he just told us to get in the car. The kids were excited about going for a ride with Uncle Bill.

I couldn't say that I knew my brother well. We had been separated for so many years. The foster care agency had arranged that one visit for us when he was twelve and I was eight. We didn't see each other again for seven years. We were only able to develop a close, loving relationship after becoming adults. I loved and admired him and he returned that love, although he seldom talked about the past.

The day was beautiful and warm; just perfect for being outdoors. I paid little attention to where we were going. I simply enjoyed this time with my brother. We crossed the bridge over the Delaware River into Philadelphia and eventually stopped at a park. A sign identified it as "Pennypack Park." We let the children run and play in the park as we sat on a bench talking.

"Let's walk for awhile," Bill said. As we exited the park on the far side, he asked, "Does this look familiar to you?"

"I have the feeling I've been here before, but I can't remember when or why."

"This is the neighborhood where we lived around the corner from each other." He pointed out his house and also the one where I had lived. A flood of unpleasant memories washed over me.

As we stood across the street, gazing at the row houses stretching to our left and right, I saw everything from a mother's perspective. My daughter was just about four years old and I would never allow her to go that far by herself. Maybe my foster mother wasn't mean or stupid, but she certainly was insensitive.

Chapter 2
Beginning Again

The day I arrived at my new foster home, was a typical cold, crisp April morning in eastern Pennsylvania. The kind of day that by afternoon the sun was bright, and the air had turned warm. A lazy feeling hung in the air that gave just a hint of the long, hot summer to come.

My childish eyes saw everything in sharp contrast. The leaves were the darkest green and the breeze rustled them gently. The sun was brilliant, and the sky was a beautiful robin's egg blue. I walked toward a parking area with a lady I did not know. She was a social worker from the foster care agency. She was not the same lady who had removed me from my previous home. I don't recall what we talked about or if we talked at all. This lady would drive me to my new, permanent foster home. Somehow, I sensed that this was a very important day.

Slowly, I made my way to where the lady's car was parked, playing a balancing game on the curb, as I carefully placed one foot in front of the other. In the cool, early morning, I could see my breath making little white puffs in the air. I pulled my little sweater closer to ward off the chill.

As we drove away, the distinct sounds of Philadelphia were clear. A boat whistle sounded from the nearby dock on the

Delaware River. An elevated train sped by overhead, making a great racket. Noisy trucks shifted slowly through their gears and a bus driver impatiently blew his horn at a motorist. Work crews shouted at one another and motorists were angry because other drivers were not moving fast enough. I had no idea where we were going or why.

The drive from downtown Philadelphia to the suburbs was a long one. I rolled the car window down and listened to the city singing as we drove underneath the elevated train tracks. For a long time, I sat quietly, trying to sort out the clamor all around me. Many years later, I heard a song by Neil Diamond titled, "Beautiful Noise." He expressed vividly in his music exactly what I heard that day.

The ride seemed to take forever. *Will we ever get there?* I was bored and sleepy. The mohair upholstery on the car seat was prickly on the back of my little legs. The raised pattern formed little rectangles on my skin. On and on we drove. Boredom took over and I traced those little boxes in the upholstery with my finger. All I wanted was to get out of that car.

All of a sudden, a sound high and clear above everything else caught my attention. At first, I couldn't identify it. It was familiar and new at the same time. It was a bird chirping! He was singing with all his might. I couldn't see him, but as I listened, I realized he wasn't the only one. He had lots of friends singing with him! They were having a grand old time.

The city noises that had kept me from hearing the birds were falling away behind us. Our surroundings were different. A softness was in the air. Everything was green: trees, bushes, lawns. Fewer cars occupied the road, and the streets were wider. I could even hear dogs barking, the rattling sounds of lawn mowers, and children laughing as they played. These were gentle, peaceful sounds that seemed to welcome me to a whole new world.

We reached our destination and the social worker parked in front of what would be my home for the next fourteen years. She must have coached me well as we drove along because I accepted that this day I was going to meet my "new" mommy. Still, my little mind questioned, *Why do I need a new mommy? I have a mommy.*

I struggled mightily to open the car door. It took both hands and feet and all my strength, but finally, the door swung open. Stepping out into the bright April sunshine, I found myself on a long walkway leading up to a big house. I walked hesitantly up the sidewalk to the foot of the porch steps. A gray-haired old woman waited on the porch with her arms folded. Braids wrapped around her head like a cap. Her skin was wrinkled, and she seemed to be about the age of my grandmother, whom I dimly remembered. She didn't smile a welcome or ask me to come in. She simply glared down at me. Suddenly, I felt uncomfortable and afraid. Yes, I had been told that this woman was my mommy now, but I didn't know her. I'd never seen her before. I stopped, tilted my head, and asked, "Mommy, can I stay out and play now?"

That day was the beginning of a new life for me; a life I regret to say was neither happy nor safe. The next fourteen years were ones of abuse of every kind, physical, verbal, emotional and even sexual.

Chapter 3
Phony

On that April day when, as a four-year-old, I entered my new home, I found it huge, dark, and frightening. The furniture was dark wood and although there were quite a few windows, the dark green window shades were always pulled partway down, which only added to the gloom. My bedroom was at the top of the stairs. It was the biggest room I'd ever had. Two big windows looked out into the backyard and our next-door neighbor's house and yard. The room contained a full-size four poster bed which was the biggest bed I'd ever had. In the daylight, it was pleasant enough and yet, for no apparent reason, I immediately felt a sense of fear. Maybe it was just because of all that had happened in the past. Everything was strange and new.

I didn't meet my foster father until that evening when he arrived home from work. He was stern and unsmiling. He simply ate his dinner, sat down in the living room, and read the evening paper. I don't remember if he even spoke to me.

At bedtime that night, my new foster mother informed me that my bedroom door would be closed and all the lights turned off. I readied myself for bed, then my foster mother said, "Goodnight," turned out the light, and walked out the door, closing it firmly behind her. There was no goodnight hug and no tucking in. She simply left me alone there in the dark. I'd never known that kind of loneliness and fear. I slept very little that night.

When I woke the next morning, I realized I'd wet the bed. I never did that. I was scared. I don't know why I was so frightened; I just knew I was in big trouble. The only thing I could think of was to hide it. I made up the bed so no one would know. Have you ever seen how a four-year-old makes a bed? They knew. I learned very quickly that I had good reason to be afraid. That was the first time I met the four-inch razor strap. It stung viciously across the back of my little legs and left dark red marks. That old razor strap was the preferred instrument of punishment for any disobedience. If I got in trouble, I was instructed to get the strap. That way I would have to think about what I did and why I was being beaten. It increased the fear.

I was lost and alone. My daddy had abandoned me. My mother had turned Billy and me over to the foster care agency. I had no hope that I'd ever see him again. Nana and Papa were no longer in my life and my aunt and uncle were gone, too.

The house was occupied by my foster parents, Bessie and Moritz, their daughter, Gladys whose nickname was Teen, and her husband, Bill. Two other foster children lived in the home. Ed was about the same age as my brother and Eleanor was about sixteen. They were all strangers to me and yet I was supposed to think of them as family.

From the beginning, no matter how hard I tried, I could not do anything to please my foster mother. I tried so hard to be good. I made up my mind to do exactly what I was told, but I always failed to measure up to her expectations. I didn't understand what had happened to me. How did I come to be here? Who were these people? Why did I have to live here? Where was my mother, my brother? I was convinced I'd been sent to this awful place because I was bad. In my mind, I was being punished simply because I wanted to go play with my big brother. No one wanted me. There must be something terribly wrong with me to make my daddy leave me. I even believed my mother sent me away because she didn't love me. Mother taught me there was a God in heaven who loved me, but even He had abandoned me.

Bedtime became a dreaded part of each day. My foster mother would tell me to go to bed. I absolutely hated going up those narrow stairs. I felt the most alone when I was in that dark bedroom night after night. For years, I would lie awake for long hours, fearful there was something or someone under the bed or in the closet just waiting for an opportunity to jump out and get me. I was afraid to move. Every night, I curled up in a tight ball with my face down in the mattress and the pillow and covers pulled over my head. My fists were tucked under me, tightly closed. I could not move for fear the monsters would pounce. I worked hard at trying to disappear. The clock in my room slowly ticked away the hours. It was often well after 2:00 a.m. when I would finally drift off to sleep.

It took me a long time to work up the courage just to go to the bathroom. I would lay there trying to tell myself that I really didn't need to get up after all. Yet, I knew I could not risk wetting the bed again. When I finally did move, I ran out of that room. Coming back, I ran and vaulted into the bed quickly before the monster under the bed would wake up and catch me.

It seems odd, but this fear began immediately upon my arrival in this home. It didn't develop with time and experience; it was there from the very beginning. There was something frightening about this house, these people. On the surface, they seemed like nice folks, but they were not.

I think I'd been in this home about two years when everyone in the family was excited and filled with anticipation because *The Philadelphia Record*, a newspaper that is now out of print, published an article about the family. The article reported about how many children the family had fostered and what a great work they were doing. There was even a staged picture of both foster parents and Ed and Eleanor gathered around the dining room table. The children were doing homework and receiving help from both parents. Everyone was smiling. I was just a little girl, and yet, I knew it was all so phony.

Chapter 4
That's Not Fair

M y foster father was cold and distant; a strict disciplinari-
an. Any disobedience or even suspected disobedience
would result in a licking across the back of my little legs with
the four-inch razor strap. He always seemed to be angry and
troubled. In later years, I came to understand he was not well
the entire the time I knew him. He had a heart condition that
took his life when I was seven. He may very well have been a
nice person; I just never saw him that way. When I was an
adult, I realized, with sadness, that I never even had a chance to
get to know the man.

Over and over my foster mother said, "Now, don't you dare
tell anyone about anything that goes on in this house. It's none
of their business." She also instructed, "You stay out of other
people's houses, do you understand?"

I was a friendly kid. I never met a stranger. I got to know
our neighbors and really enjoyed talking with them. There was
Mrs. Hipple and Frankie, the lady who lived next to her. Mrs.
Hipple was a kind lady who spoke softly. Frankie, whom all the
kids called, "Aunt Frankie," was just as loud as Mrs. Hipple was
quiet. The Sloatmans were very kind and always happy to give
us apples from their trees. Then there was dear Mrs. Gilcrest.

She was elderly. I think she really liked me. We enjoyed sitting on her porch talking. She was a widow and lived by herself in a big house. As young as I was, I could tell she was very lonely.

One hot summer day Mrs. Gilcrest told me she had made fresh lemonade. She invited me to come inside and have some. I knew it was against the rules. If I got caught, I would be in big trouble. *I don't think a few minutes will matter.* No one would know. The thought of fresh, ice cold lemonade made my mouth water. It was so very tempting. I followed her inside. Even now, I can remember how wonderful that lemonade tasted.

We were probably in the house ten minutes or so. I felt nervous and scared the whole time, yet I enjoyed being in her house. It was dark and cool inside. Mrs. Gilcrest had lots of old furniture and pretty, lacy doilies covering tables and the backs of her chairs and sofa. The nice smell of furniture polish hung in the air and the floors were really shiny. I was relieved, however, when we walked back out onto the porch. It was after five o'clock.

Unfortunately, at that very moment, my foster father was walking down the street on his way home from work. He looked up and saw me coming out of Mrs. Gilcrest's house. He told me to get in the house right away and sure enough, I had to go get the razor strap. I remember thinking that I had not done anything wrong. What was the harm in having a glass of lemonade with a friend? It made no sense, and it wasn't fair. Frequently, through the early years I was in foster care, my little heart and mind would be totally outraged at the unfairness of it all. This was one of those times when that little voice in my head was practically screaming, *Why are adults so mean and unfair?*

Visits from my mother were a bright spot in my life. She couldn't come often, because of her work schedule, but when I was with her, I knew I was loved. She made sure I knew she was trying very hard to save enough money so Billy and I could come live with her again. We talked about that possibility often.

Aunt Emma, mother's sister, was four years older than Mother. She and Uncle Bill had one daughter. I loved my cousin, Joan. She was about five years older than I. When we were together, which was seldom, we always had fun. In the years I lived in this home, there were maybe three or four times when on a Sunday afternoon, Aunt Emma and Uncle Bill drove Mother to the suburbs to visit me. This saved her a long trip on public transportation. I loved those visits. Joan and I played outside while the adults sat on the porch and drank iced tea and talked. These were rare times when I actually felt I belonged to my family. Most of the time, I felt all alone. I believed no one wanted me.

Joan and I did a lot of laughing and acting silly. Frequently, the adults were the subject of our silliness. It was obvious that Aunt Emma was in charge and she regularly told Uncle Bill how things were. Joan was well aware of this relationship between her dad and her mom and she would make funny comments about it. I didn't notice it so much as a child, but as I got older, I began to see that Aunt Emma also had a good deal of control over my mother.

Aunt Emma told me several times about when they were children. She said, "Your mother was so cute. She charmed everyone. People came to visit and they fussed over her. The first thing they asked was if Millie would sing a song. She was always the center of attention. Then they told me, 'Emma, go put the kettle on for tea.' I always thought of myself as Polly put the kettle on."

As I grew older, I became aware of a jealousy Aunt Emma had toward my mother. It seemed that Aunt Emma acted more like my mother's parent, rather than her sister. But, I was a child and I really didn't care about all this adult stuff. I was only interested in having fun with my cousin.

All too soon, it was time for my family to head back to the city. Mother hugged me and told me she'd see me soon. Then they all climbed into the car and waved goodbye. It was always such a letdown for me. Once again, I was alone and desolate. I took refuge in my bedroom.

Chapter 5
Losing "Daddy"

Summer in Eastern Pennsylvania was usually miserable. We often had ninety-eight degree temperatures and ninety-eight percent humidity. Houses were not yet equipped with air conditioning, so I couldn't wait for summer to get over. I longed for autumn and the first frost. It was too hot to be outside during the day and I spent most of my time in my room. I had no energy and neither did anyone else.

My foster father was greatly affected by the weather. Even I could see the weariness in him. His face was very pale. This man went to work every day and never complained, in spite of his heart condition. He trudged home from the bus stop after a long day at work, ate his dinner, and read his paper. He never had much to say. I called my foster father "Daddy" because it was expected, although I could never think of him as . . . my daddy.

My foster mother and father had what must have been a long-standing tradition. He fixed breakfast for her every Sunday morning. When breakfast was ready, he came to the foot of the stairs and hollered, "Hey, old lady! Old lady, your breakfast is ready. You hear me old lady, get on down here!" If she didn't come down right away, then he came to the foot of the stairs and did the same thing all over again. I thought how terrible and mean he was, yelling at her like that. However, as I got older, I realized that this must have been a bit of sideways humor; a sort of game they played. It gave them a humanness I seldom saw. Perhaps they actually did care for one another.

One stifling hot Sunday night when I was seven years old, I could not sleep. Not a single breath of air stirred, but there was more activity in the house than usual. Family members were going up and down the steps. I could hear hushed and urgent conversations. Somewhere around 9:00 p.m., I overheard my foster mother say, "I think we need to call the doctor."

After a while, I heard all the adults coming up the stairs with the doctor. I easily identified the voices of Moritz (Bus), my foster parents' oldest son, and Joe, the youngest. Gladys (Teen) was the oldest of their three children and Bill was her husband. The doctor's voice was different; calm and reassuring. When he arrived, the house became quieter. I didn't hear much running up and down the steps after that. I heard bits of conversation but could not make out what was being said. I sensed something was terribly wrong.

Later, my foster mother shuffled down the hallway. I crept out of bed and opened the door. "What's happening?"

She shooed me back into the room. "It's nothing for you to concern yourself with. Go back to bed. You should be asleep."

"I've been trying, but it's so hot and there's so much noise. What's happening?"

She was upset, and I noticed tears in her eyes. I could tell she was in a hurry to get back to the front bedroom. She did not want to be bothered with a scared little kid. She yelled, "Get back in that bed and keep this door closed."

I did what I was told. I knew better than to argue or disobey. As I turned back into my room, I peeked down the hall. Teen, Bill and the doctor were gathered around the bed. My foster father was lying in the bed. I had often been told that he was not well and I shouldn't bother him, but no one ever told me how sick he really was. He looked so small and frail. I was struck with an awful sense of dread and fear.

I knew if I didn't do what I was told I would be in trouble. I didn't want to risk a beating with the razor strap. I tried to block out the noise and fear so I could go to sleep, but it wasn't possible. The hot, humid, dark night dragged on and on.

Around 5:00 a.m., I heard a stirring. Again, I could not hear what was said, but the doctor mumbled something, and I heard his footsteps coming down the hall and then on the steps. I heard his car start and pull away from the curb. It got very quiet in the house. All off a sudden, I heard weeping. It was an awful, heart-wrenching sound. My foster mother sobbed as if her heart were breaking. I felt so bad and wished there was something I could do for her. I lived with her for fourteen years and this was the only time I ever heard her cry. I wanted to open my bedroom door so I could see down the hall, but I didn't dare. Even as a seven-year-old child, I was able to figure out that my foster father had died. I lay awake for a long time, listening to the sounds of sadness and grief coming from the front room, wondering what I should do next. After a while, my eyelids got too heavy to stay open and I slipped into a deep, dreamless sleep.

The next morning, I came downstairs quietly, not knowing what to expect. I imagined I'd find all kinds of activities going on and lots of people there. My foster mother was alone in the kitchen just as she was every morning. She'd cooked breakfast and was busy tidying up and washing dishes. Teen and Bill had evidently gone to work. I was stunned. It was like any ordinary day. I had no idea what to say or do.

Finally, she said, "Sit down and get ready for breakfast." She said nothing else. I kept waiting for her to sit down by me and tell me about Daddy, but she didn't say a word. The silence was awful. It dragged on and on. Finally, I couldn't keep still any longer.

"Daddy died last night, didn't he?"

"Yes, he did." That was all she said.

I sat down at the table and turned my attention to eating my breakfast. I didn't want to get in any trouble, but I desperately wanted to tell her I'd heard her crying and I was so sorry. The words just wouldn't come. She'd often told me, "In this house, children are to be seen and not heard." So, I was too afraid to say anything else.

I was sheltered from all the preparations and events that accompanied Daddy's death. Children did not go to funerals. It was all so strange. My foster father had just disappeared, never to return. I felt a sense of sadness, but I could not grieve for a man I hardly knew.

Chapter 6
A New Friend

I did not live in this home very long before I learned that my foster mother had little use for anyone who was "different." People of different racial backgrounds, religions, and nationalities were all suspect in her view. She categorized everyone with the slang terms of the times. Most of these were not complimentary. If you were not white, of European background, and Methodist, you were dirt as far as she was concerned. Although she never went to church herself, she believed the Methodist Church was the only "correct" one.

We never went to church as a family. Instead, she sent me to church and Sunday school. It didn't matter what church it was. Sometimes I went alone. Sometimes it was the Methodist church just up the street. At other times, I was a Lutheran or a Presbyterian, depending on where my current friend attended. Attending church was just another excuse for me to get away from the house. Bessie would give me a few coins tied up in the corner of a white handkerchief for the collection. I was never allowed any spending money. I have to confess that I'd put some coins in the collection plate as it was passed, and I'd also take some coins out. The candy store was on my way home.

In second grade, I met a new friend. She was new at school and we just seemed to hit it off. We played together at recess and ate lunch together. Our seats were near one another in the classroom. We laughed and played with our other classmates and I never even noticed the color of her skin. Few black people lived in our town and the few who did all seemed to live in an area we called "The Projects."

Now that I think about it, I guess things in the North weren't all that much different than in the South in those days. Oh, I don't remember any white and negro restrooms or fountains, but it was very clear that the two groups did not intermingle much. You know, I can't even remember this little girl's name, but it didn't matter what color our skin was. I helped her learn her way around the school and showed her where the cafeteria and the auditorium were.

One day, school dismissed early, and we walked home together. She had a good bit farther to go than I did, but we weren't in any hurry. When we came to my house, by mutual consent, we squatted on our haunches and started playing in the dirt. We were just two little kids, using sticks to write in the dirt, our heads close together as we concentrated on our work.

I didn't see my foster mother coming; never heard her approach. Suddenly, I was yanked to my feet by my upper arm and ordered to get myself in the house, right now!

"You get out of here and go on home where you belong," she said to my friend. "We don't want your kind around here, you little *%#*@!"

Bessie's words broke my heart.

I received quite a tongue lashing that day. I don't remember everything my foster mother said, but I figured out quickly that

I had been bad for befriending that little girl. The main thing that bothered my foster mother so much was that we had our heads so close together. She kept coming back to that over and over. She declared that all of "those people" have lice and she didn't want to deal with that. I don't remember my friendship with that little girl continuing. I don't think she was in my class very long. I looked for her, but I just didn't see her after that.

I do know this much. My foster mother was never able to teach me her prejudices. It seemed as if I purposely went the other way. I have tried to always accept people for who they are, not what they look like or what church they attend.

My foster mother told me there was a God and He saw everything bad that I ever did or thought about doing. He knew all my rebellious thoughts. He was a God of Judgment! She told me He walked in the storms, and the thunder I heard was His voice. I was frightened to death of thunderstorms. That was all I knew of God. Yet, when I went to church, and heard the organ play, and saw those beautiful stained-glass windows, somehow, I could not accept what my foster mother told me about Him. Did He live in those big churches? In the scenes of the stained-glass windows, He appeared so gentle and loving. Even so, I was still afraid of Him.

I loved my third grade Sunday school teacher at Norwood Methodist Church. She was young and pretty and so very loving and gentle. Her name was Mary Ann Coggin and she always greeted us with joy. She really loved her Sunday school kids. Mary Ann taught us Bible stories and made them seem so real and lifelike. She was the first person who told me that God loved me. Even more important to me at the time, though, was that I knew that she loved me.

Chapter 7
The Red Sweater

Through those early years in foster care, one of my greatest frustrations was the length of time between my mother's visits. Often, it was three months or more. Sometimes, it was closer to six months. I was always so glad to see her, and she was happy to see me. We enjoyed one another and always had fun when we were together. I could not understand why she came so infrequently. I wanted her to come every week.

When I was older, she explained that during those years, she worked six days a week at the telephone company. The trip from the city to where I lived was very long. It required a trolley ride, followed by an even longer bus trip. She had never learned to drive and could not afford a car. With just one day off a week, she was unable to visit often. She also had to make time to visit with my brother, Billy. He lived fifteen miles north of Center City, Philadelphia, while I was a good fifteen miles south the city.

There were no other foster kids in our neighborhood. None of my friends had been through anything like I was experiencing. Being "different" was the worst thing a kid could be, and I was well aware that I was different from all my friends. I often faced blunt exchanges like these:

"Why is your name different than your mother's?"

"She's not my real mother, she's my foster mother."

"What's a foster mother?"

"Well, it's someone who takes care of you when your own parents can't."

"Then, why do you call her mother?"

"Because she wants me to."

"Why can't your parents take care of you?"

"They are divorced."

"Where's your father?"

"I don't know; he just went away."

"Did he die?"

"No, he went to live somewhere else."

"Were you bad? Is that why he went away?"

Kids ask blunt questions simply because they just want answers about things they don't understand. They don't get the nuances involved in asking gently and sparing someone's feelings. Divorce was not a common thing at that time. In fact, if someone did divorce, it was often hushed up within the family and was not talked about openly. All of my school friends and the neighborhood kids had a mom and a dad all their lives. Most of them had lived in the same house since they were born. Frequently, their grandparents also lived with them. My situation was really odd to my friends. I always felt left out and alone. I yearned to be part of a normal family. When my friends ran to meet their folks at school functions or at the end of a day, I walked home . . . alone.

Bessie and my real mother were both extremely talented. Bessie crocheted beautifully, although I really didn't appreciate it at the time. She often spent her late afternoons or evenings crocheting. She would sit near the window where the light was best, and her gnarled hands were never still.

"Idle hands are the devil's workshop," she'd say frequently.

It seemed to me that her motions were automatic. She used a pattern from time to time, but for the most part, she worked without one. The crochet hooks she used were the little thin ones. The result was beautiful, tiny, intricate patterns. She made bedspreads, doilies, tablecloths, and scarves. They all looked perfect.

While I admired her work, it never meant much to me personally because I was never the beneficiary of any of these beautiful things. When I became an adult and really could appreciate the beautiful work and all the effort that went into all those handcrafted items, I wondered what had become of them. I knew that she kept many of them in a cedar chest, wrapped in tissue. She used some of the items every day, but it was sad that so many of them never saw the light of day and were never really used and enjoyed.

My dolly had a soft body and a very pretty little face. Sometimes I played with her and other times I forgot all about her. I can't remember if I ever got around to giving her a name. Sometimes, during Christmas, my dolly would disappear. I hardly noticed she was gone, but on Christmas morning, there she would be, all decked out in a brand new crocheted outfit. When the novelty wore off and I was distracted by other playmates, my dolly disappeared again. I didn't figure this out until years later. The only other Christmas gift I can remember receiving from my foster parents is a Christmas stocking filled with candy, oranges, apples, nuts, and crayons.

We never had a lot of money, but we were fed well, and I always had warm clothes—even if they were hand-me-downs from my foster brother. I had a plaid winter jacket that I hated because it was a boy's jacket. It was wool, and it made me itch. I also owned a pair of Sunday shoes and a pair of school shoes. When school was out, my school shoes became my play shoes and I started school with my Sunday shoes. Then, I got a new pair of Sunday shoes.

My birth mother gave me handknitted gifts, some of which she made on the long bus ride to visit me. I have several afghans in my cedar chest today that she made for me. I wrapped them in tissue paper to protect them because I treasured them. Isn't that ironic? They are my only connection to her now. Mother was an artist with knitting needles. I was in awe of her ability to create such perfection.

My birthday is in early October. I remember it as a non-event. My mother sent me a birthday gift, but it was always late. I cannot remember receiving any birthday gifts my foster mother. We never celebrated my special day. She didn't bake any birthday cakes for me. A party was out of the question. That cost money. Besides, a party would mean a houseful of noisy children.

One year, however, was really special. I was in third grade. First of all, Mother's visit came very close to my birthday—not on the exact day, but close. That, in and of itself, was like a birthday present. As always, I was at the bus stop waiting excitedly. I loved to see her smile as she always did when she saw me. On this particular occasion, I knew she had a present in her bag, but she laughed when I asked to see it.

"No, you have to wait," she said.

I was so excited! Mother always brought me really neat stuff. Story Bock Dolls were beautiful little dolls portraying the main characters in children's stories. Mother made sure I had a collection of them. She bought me so many books. I loved them all. There were the *Bobbsey Twins,* and as I got a little older, *The Call of the Wild,* and *White Fang.* I read all of Albert Payson Terhune's books about his collies. *My Friend Flicka* was followed by *Thunderhead, Son of Flicka.* As I got a bit older, I devoured *The Red Badge of Courage.* My mother made sure I had plenty to read. I was certain that this new present was very special.

We walked to my house together, holding hands. It was comforting to walk with her hand in mine. I kept craning my neck, trying to see what was in the bag she carried. She would have none of it. She asked me about school and told me about her work. We talked and laughed all the way past the park and down the street to my house.

Finally, we arrived at the house and she allowed me to open the tissue wrapped package. It was soft. *What could it be?* It seemed to me it was going to take all afternoon to get that wrapping undone. When I peeled back the last of the paper, I let out a gasp of surprise and joy. My mother knitted me a bright red, cable stitch sweater and it didn't matter one bit that it was late. It was such a beautiful sweater. I was so very proud of it! I couldn't wait to tell all my friends that my mother had made it for me. I had never received a gift that made me feel so special. I was somebody! *My mommy really does love me!*

To this day, I can recall that sweater. I remember the feel of it; the softness and warmth of the thick yarn. The color was the brightest red and it went perfectly with my dark curls and eyes.

I could hardly wait for the next day so that I could wear it to school. Instantly it became my most prized possession.

I was able to proudly say to all my friends, "My real mommy made this for me." For a time, all the questions they were always asking were silenced. The other kids understood that I did have a real mother who loved me. I was proud every time I wore that sweater. I refused to give it up, even when it became worn and too small. Even though I couldn't wear it anymore, I kept it for a long time. Even today, red is probably my best color. I have to confess, if I ever see a red, cable knit sweater that even resembles the one my mother made, I will pay any price for it.

Ironically, that sweater became the catalyst for a deep depression and sadness that led to my most significant adventure. Maybe I should say "misadventure."

Chapter 8
The Runaway

By the time I was eight, Ed, my next oldest foster brother and I were the only ones still in the home. Verbal abuse was a part of my everyday life. My foster mother was cold and cruel. She never seemed to miss an opportunity to say something hurtful. I often wished I had a nickel for every time I heard, "Oh, you can't do anything right!" She told me over and over, "You will never amount to anything." It was like an endless song beating its cadence into my head, day after day. I felt totally worthless.

Bessie became especially irritable and critical whenever my mother came to visit. I was always excited and happy on those days. Yet, Bessie always spoiled everything. The minute I got back to the house from walking my mother to the bus stop, she would start in on me. She would say, "Every time your mother comes to visit you act like that." She never explained what "like that" actually meant. I had no idea what I did that caused her to be so angry. I was well into adulthood before I realized that my foster mother was jealous of my mother.

That beautiful red sweater my mother made for me became a catalyst. It was an assurance of my mother's love and it became a thread of hope to which I could cling. My heart spilled over with love for her. I thought constantly about being with my mother. I missed her so very much. I needed to know more about where she went after she climbed onto the bus and left me, so one day I asked her.

She explained that the bus went to a town called, Darby.

I pressed her further. "Then what?"

She told me she went to the trolley station down the hill and got on a trolley that took her into Philadelphia.

"What trolley?"

"The Number 11."

She never asked why I was asking and I don't think I was even fully aware of the plan beginning to form in my mind. I was a kid and it never occurred to me to ask her for her address or phone number.

Norwood Elementary School, where I attended, had a school cafeteria, but we couldn't afford to buy lunches there, so all of us carried our lunches in a brown, paper bag. We didn't call them sacks; that was too fancy a name. Usually, I had a peanut butter and jelly sandwich wrapped in waxed paper and an orange or an apple for lunch. Of course, that meant by lunch time there was a big hole in the middle of my sandwich because the orange or apple would be crunched up against it. I'm sure I was not too gentle carrying that paper bag. Occasionally, we did have bologna as a special treat. The bologna sandwich always had mayonnaise, which tasted good, but it also made the bread slip and slide all over the place while I was eating it.

In my imagination, I pictured myself walking away, past my school, going straight to the bus stop. I could just disappear, and no one would care. Each day, I was given seven cents for a carton of milk. I devised a plan to save all that money for a long time. I drank water and hoarded my milk money for ten whole days. I was convinced that I had a lot of money and so one day, I put my plan into action.

As I walked past my school, I dropped my arithmetic book (it wasn't called math then) at the entrance and continued walking the extra block to the bus stop. My heart pounded in my chest; I was so scared. After a short, nervous wait, the bus came. I hopped on and rode all the way to Darby. I wasn't frightened anymore. I knew where to go; my mother had told me. I reasoned that my foster mother wouldn't even care that I was gone. I was certain she'd be glad to be rid of me.

As the bus pulled into Darby, I opened my hand and looked at the money I had left. I was amazed at how much of my little stash was taken up by the bus fare. I knew I would not have enough to pay for the trolley. Now I felt real fear. The bus stopped, and I got off and stood on the sidewalk, bewildered. *What should I do?*

An elderly lady was sweeping her sidewalk and she looked my way. My face must have shown panic. Without even thinking about it, I turned on the tears. She came over to me and asked what was wrong. I knew if I told the truth, I would be on the way back to Norwood and in big trouble. Without even planning it, I lied. Boy, did I tell a whopper! Between my sobs, I concocted a story on the spur of the moment.

"I'm supposed to meet my mommy in Philadelphia because I have a dentist appointment. I've lost my money." The lady gave me a dollar! That was a lot of money!

Then she questioned me closely. "Are you sure you know where to go?"

I assured her I did. I pointed down the hill to where we could see the trolley station and said, "I go down there and get the Number 11."

That answer satisfied her, and she told me to go ahead. She stood there watching me as I started off down the hill. This lady I had never met and would never see again was so kind to me. I turned around to smile and wave to her and she waved back. I did not feel even a twinge of guilt for my deception. I felt safe and protected because this lady cared enough to stand there and watch until I got safely down the hill.

By the time I got to the trolley station, my confidence had returned. I had enough money for the fare and I was going to find my mother. I was eight years old. I had no idea how big Philadelphia was. I did not have my mother's address or phone number. I found the Number 11 trolley and hopped aboard like I knew what I was doing. The trolley started off and I was comfortable and confident. Soon, I would be with my mother forever.

I'd been riding a long time when I looked ahead and saw a huge tunnel opening. I had never even heard of a subway-surface car. Down and down we went down into that deep, dark tunnel. I was as scared as I'd ever been in my life. I knew that God had heard my awful lie and was taking me to that terrible place of punishment that Bessie often warned me about.

I had no idea where to get off and so I sat still. People came and went and still, I rode. I had no plan. I was sure I would see my mother on one of the platforms as the train came to a stop. The car stopped every few minutes and I scanned the faces in the crowds for a glimpse of my mother, but I couldn't find her. So, I just stayed glued to my seat. The car became more and more crowded. Finally, around 5:15 p.m., I decided I had to get off and try to find my mother. At the next stop, I left the trolley and just stood on the platform looking around, trying to read the signs. I didn't know where I was or what to do next. My heart was pounding.

A strange man approached me. He was a quiet, friendly man. Even though I knew I was not to talk to strangers, somehow, I immediately trusted him. He was dressed in a business suit and tie and his voice was quiet and gentle when he asked if he could help me. I told him that I was trying to find my mother who lived in Philadelphia. He asked me for her address. Then he asked if I had her phone number. I hung my head. The next thing I knew, I was in a police station. He was a plain-clothes police officer. I felt betrayed when they called my foster mother.

At 11:00 p.m., Bessie and I were driving back to Norwood in the old 1941 Plymouth. I had traveled all day. I had gone from approximately fifteen miles south of Philadelphia to the North Philadelphia train station. That was fifteen miles north of the city. Without too much trouble, I could easily have been on my way to New York City.

A heavy silence filled the car as my foster mother drove us back to Norwood. I was certain I was going to be killed for this escapade.

Finally, Bessie spoke to me in a clipped, angry voice. "I suppose you think you're going to get a good licking for this?"

I could not speak for the lump in my throat, so I just nodded.

"Well, the agency and I have spoken, and we feel that you have been through quite enough for one day and a licking will not be necessary this time."

I was so shocked I almost collapsed on the floor of the car. I could hardly believe my ears. We didn't talk the rest of the way home. She didn't even ask why I ran away. I assumed she didn't care.

The next day, I was informed that a visitor was coming to talk with me. That was our pet name for social workers. Oh boy, I was really in trouble now! I learned later that the agency was in a real lather about this incident. This was major stuff. They had a runner and they wanted to get to the bottom of the matter.

All the social workers who came to visit were stamped from the same mold. Usually, they were older women, wearing gray flannel business suits and clunky shoes. Most of them wore their hair in a bun. They all sounded the same, too. We never had the same one for very long. I knew they weren't interested in me at all. They just wanted to make sure that each of their cases perked along smoothly and there were no bumps in the road. Heaven forbid that anyone should rock their little boat in any way. I was a runner and that was not acceptable.

As I waited for the visitor to arrive, my thoughts were only about how much trouble I was in. I knew I would be moved to a different home and I had no expectation that it would be a change for the better. I was sure it would be a terrible place; possibly an orphanage with a bunch of other worthless kids just like me.

When the car finally pulled up to the curb, I watched with little interest until I noticed that the woman exiting the vehicle was not at all what I was expecting. She was not old. Her hair wasn't arranged in a bun; it was short and fluffy and framed her face in an attractive way. She was even dressed attractively. No gray flannel suit here. She wore an easy smile as she came up the walk and into the house.

Introductions were made and then she made the big announcement: "Carole and I are going to go out in the car and talk for a while."

Well now, I knew what that meant. She'd talk, I'd listen. I was one angry little girl. I'd show her! I would not say a word! I decided that I would not even listen to her. These people were all alike! My resentment was in full bloom.

We sat in the car and I remember it being a pleasant, cool afternoon. The late afternoon sun felt warm and comforting. The breeze drifted in through the open windows. She started to talk, and I just turned off my brain. I don't know how long she talked. It could have been five minutes, or ten, I'm not sure, but there was a point when the tone of her voice, or her words, began to penetrate my little wall. She sounded really concerned about me. She was saying something to the effect that if I was really that unhappy here, maybe we could see about having me transferred to another home.

I could not believe what I was hearing. Did I dare trust this lady? Could I believe her when she said she really cared? I was not sure any adult could be trusted to mean what he or she said.

Unhappy? Did they think I'd run away just for the fun of it? The only person I trusted was my mother and the only thing I wanted was to be with her. I felt like I didn't belong to anyone and no one wanted me except my mother.

Suddenly, everything that was pent up inside me came tumbling out. I told her how I'd planned my trip to Philadelphia for a long time. I blurted it all out. I told her everything, all about the physical punishment and how nothing I did was right. As hard as I tried to be good, it seemed to me I was always in trouble. I spent lots of time in my bedroom, where I was supposed to be thinking about my bad behavior. Bessie lost no opportunity to declare loudly over and over how dumb I was.

"Carole, you just can't seem to keep your head about you."

I didn't understand what that meant, and no one bothered to explain it to me. My head went with me everywhere I went, didn't it? I was constantly reminded me that I would never amount to anything. I actually believed Bessie would be glad when I ran away to Philadelphia. I was surprised that anyone even bothered to look for me.

After we'd talked for a long time, the social worker said she had to get back to the office. As we got ready to return to the house, cautioned me not to expect miracles. "These things take time and I can't change things in a week or two. You will have to be patient, but I will see what I can do." Her words gave me hope for the first time.

By this time, I loved this lady. She spoke gently and smiled a lot. I would have gone with her at that very moment, but I had to stay where I was for now. As I watched her drive away, I felt content. I knew that her next planned visit was in six months. I could wait that long because I trusted her to bring me good news.

Six months later when my foster mother told me that a visitor would be coming, I could hardly wait. The morning of her visit, I paced back and forth from the front door to the windows that looked out on the street. I went out on the porch and checked again and again for the gray sedan that I knew would be coming soon. I was dressed up in a clean skirt, blouse, and saddle shoes. I wanted to make a good impression. It seemed as if time stood still, but finally, the car pulled up to the curb in front of our house. The suspense was awful as I waited for my friend to open the car door.

"Oh, no. That is not her!"

The lady who stepped out of the car was old! She had a bun in her hair and was wearing a gray business suit. Besides that, she had a thick German accent and I could hardly understand her. She had a long German name that I could not pronounce. From the moment I saw her, she didn't stand a chance with me. My little wall went right up again. When I timidly asked about my friend, she said sharply, "Oh, she has been reassigned."

The anger and disappointment that welled up in me was inexpressible. Inside, I was ranting and raving, screaming in rage at my friend's betrayal. At least, I thought she was my friend. I knew for certain now that I could not trust any adult, especially social workers. With the exception of my mother, I was closed mouthed and wary from then on whenever I was with an adult. They lied! They all lied! That's just what adults did. I gave up all hope of a new home and for the second time in my few short years, I knew despair.

Chapter 9
Grundy

World War II finally ended. When it was safe enough to travel overseas, my foster sister, Teen, went to Germany to be with her husband, Bill. He was an Army lieutenant, assigned to the 1st Infantry Division, a unit that was dubbed the Big Red One. Bill was stationed in Nuremberg, Germany, serving as a guard at the Nuremberg trials. He was a canine officer. Teen happened to be the second American spouse to walk down the gangplank into Germany.

I missed my foster sister, Teen, so much. Her real name was Gladys, but she had picked up the nickname Teen. She was the only member of the family who cared anything about me. Months later, when they came home, Teen and Bill lived with us.

Teen took me aside one afternoon. "We've got a big surprise coming."

"Really?" I asked. "What is it?"

"Oh, now, you know I can't tell you. It would spoil the surprise. You'll just have to wait and see."

Almost nine months passed before the big day. It took all that time to make the arrangements. I must have driven Teen crazy asking over and over about the big surprise.

One day, a large truck pulled up in front of our house. The men on the truck very carefully offloaded a huge wooden crate. They went to work opening the crate with crowbars and screwdrivers. Finally, the box was opened, and a wooden gangplank was set at the opening. We stood watching intently. The tension was almost a physical thing. Then a gorgeous dog stepped out. I was mesmerized, and immediately in love. He was so big that he almost stood to my chest.

His name was Grundy and he was the most beautiful creature I'd ever seen. A German Shepherd, born and bred in Germany, he stepped into my life when I was nine. I was desperate for a friend. In the five years I'd lived in this foster home, this was the first time I found real joy in anything.

At first, though, I was too scared to even approach him, but Grundy was quiet and gentle. His coat was long and thick and ever so soft. When Teen spoke gently to him and told him it was okay, he came right to me. He must have been groomed before he was brought to our house because he smelled so clean. I just wanted to bury my face in his thick fur. He was mostly black but there were tan and white markings on the underside of his body, tail, and paws. His tail was a huge plume which he insisted on carrying over his back. A German Shepherd is correctly supposed to carry his tail down.

Grundy's most striking feature, however, was his necklace. It started with a white spot on his neck. After that came rings of color: tan, white, black, and gray. Ring after ring went all the way down to the top of his front paws. He looked like a king wearing a decorated chest protector. All the kids in the neighborhood gathered around to see this awesome sight.

Grundy settled into our lives. He was a dog you could hug and pounce on. He loved it. TV was in its early years and our screen was just a little black and white square. My brothers and sisters and I made Grundy lie down on his side and we'd use him for a TV pillow. He never moved until we did. He was so patient and never seemed to tire of us. Grundy was even gentle with our cat, Baby. There was some concern about the initial meeting between the two animals, but we needn't have worried. Grundy and Baby got along just fine.

Grundy was bred and trained to be a military law enforcement dog. He finished his basic training and was placed in more specialized work. That is how he ended up in Nuremberg. Bill was his handler. It was Army policy to never transfer a dog to a new handler, so when Bill was discharged, he was given permission to bring Grundy home.

Grundy only understood commands in German. He had to be taught the English commands equivalent to the German ones he already knew. Sometimes we'd use the German words and sometimes English. "Essen" meant "eat." He never forgot that one. "Nix" was "no." He obeyed every command instantly. Even his pedigree papers were in German. His registered name was "Neander Vonder Veda Varda" (I think that's pretty close). I remember thinking, "No wonder they call him Grundy."

My greatest joy came when Teen allowed me to take Grundy to the park by myself. She had taught me how to handle him, carefully explaining the proper positions for each of the commands. At the park, I put him through his paces: "Heel. Sit. Stay. Lie down. Come." I think I was showing off, just a little. Grundy did not move or change position until I gave him a new command.

"Grundy, down!" Immediately he dropped to the ground with his head up and ears forward, anticipating the next command.

"Stay." I turned and walked away leaving him lying there on the ground for long periods of time. He never moved.

"Grundy, come!" He came and sat right in front of me.

"Heel." He moved around to my left side and sat, waiting.

Grundy and I received some strange looks from folks in the park. I guess they were surprised to see a giant of a dog walking so easily with this little kid. Sometimes, people asked me how I was able to handle such a huge, fierce looking animal. I was so proud! I pretended he was my dog. I was honored to be trusted with him. I'd never loved anything or anyone like I did Grundy. For the first time in my life, I began to understand unconditional love.

Grundy's diet consisted of fresh horsemeat, cooked with cabbage and other vegetables. It required cooking for several hours and it smelled up the whole house.

"Wow, that stuff smells so bad. I don't know how he can eat it!" I exclaimed.

"Dogs prefer different smells than humans." Teen laughed.

She allowed me to help by feeding him and checking to make sure he had plenty of water. I helped brush him, too. He was so big and his fur so thick. It really was quite a job, although he always stood perfectly still. Teen explained that German bred shepherds were long haired, while the American bred shepherds had shorter hair.

Summers were so hot and humid in Eastern Pennsylvania. I remember switching places on my bed frequently during the night because the fresh place on the sheet was nice and cool for a bit. Grundy had a hard time, too. During the night, he'd climb into the porcelain bathtub to get cool. I never got used to coming into the bathroom half asleep and seeing this big, black, furry thing filling the tub. I jumped every time. I laughed at myself every time, too. *Oh, it's only Grundy trying to keep cool.*

Chapter 10
Wolf

Bill turned Grundy's shipping crate into a dog house. However, Grundy refused to go inside it. He was always on top of it. I guess he'd had enough of being inside it during the trip from Germany. Bill screwed a huge metal eyelet into the front of the crate and attached a long, heavy chain to it. This gave Grundy a good bit of freedom to move around.

Grundy never growled except for that low rumble in his throat when we were playing tug of war with a toy. However, he did have one little flaw. While always gentle with little animals, he could not tolerate a dog his size or larger. His ego got in the way.

A neighbor across the street owned a dog named Wolf who was almost as big as Grundy. He was a mutt who sort of resembled a German Shepherd. Wolf broke loose often, and where do you think he headed? He came directly to our yard with challenge on his mind. I think both dogs understood who the better dog was.

My brothers and sisters and I were warned often to never get between Wolf and Grundy. Several "almost" fights erupted, but the adults managed to separate the two and send Wolf on his way. I can't remember how many times I'd have to yell from the backyard, "Teen, Bill, Mom . . . Wolf's in the yard again! He and Grundy are going to fight!"

Wolf knew how to frustrate Grundy. He understood that Grundy was restrained and that he would not be able to chase after him. Wolf always stayed just out of reach, acting almost like a kid taunting another. He seemed to be saying, "Hahaha, I'm loose and you're tied up." Grundy was not only smart, but he was also strong. He ran to the end of his chain and lunged, over and over again. Pretty soon, his dog house moved just a little. As he continued to lunge and pull hard, he managed to get the dog house to the grass, where it would begin to slide. Pretty soon he was pulling it along as if he were pulling a sled. He hauled that dog house through the side yard and onto the front lawn. From there, he simply continued pulling until he got that thing across the street. He was going to get Wolf. The only thing that stopped Grundy was the curb on the other side of the street. That was where Teen and Bill would catch him.

A couple who lived on the street behind us were friends with Teen and Bill. They owned a beautiful Great Dane who stood a head taller than Grundy. One afternoon, that dog made the mistake of walking into our yard when Grundy was not tied up. Grundy looked small compared to that Great Dane, but I was practically rolling on the ground laughing as the scene unfolded. Grundy took one look at that dog and chased him right out of the yard. It was like watching two giants; the smaller one in hot pursuit of the larger. The Dane never came back.

Every week the family gathered around the TV to watch *The Original Amateur Hour*. On one of the episodes, there was a performing dog. As part of the act, the dog said, "Mamma" as clear as could be.

Bill turned to Grundy and said, "You dummy, why aren't you that smart?"

I never thought anything more about it.

My foster mother, however, took his remark as a challenge. When I arrived home from school the next day, there she was, sitting in her favorite chair by the living room window. Grundy was sitting in front of her. As I came into the room, she said, "Watch this." Turning to Grundy, she commanded, "Say, Grandmom."

My jaw dropped when Grundy said, "Grandmom."

"How did you teach him to do that?"

"Grundy and I spent the day together."

My foster mother was always busy with laundry, cooking, or cleaning. When she wasn't doing housework, she was crocheting. Knowing she had taken one entire day and used up a whole lot of doggie snacks just to prove her son-in-law wrong made me laugh out loud. That day, I saw a side of my foster mother I'd never seen before; a softer side.

When Teen and Bill got home, my foster mother called everyone into the living room. Then she called Grundy and had him sit in front of her. She commanded him to say "Grandmom."

Everyone was stunned, except me, of course.

From then on, whenever Grundy got a snack, he always said "Grandmom" first.

Chapter 11
Fluffy

People sometimes make comparisons between dogs and their owners. I've read articles in which the owner is described as looking like the dog, or the dog behaves like the owner. Our next-door neighbor fit that profile perfectly. She was a bit on the snooty side. As long as things went her way, everything was fine, but she could be quite snippy when they didn't. Her dark hair was rather coarse and streaked with gray. Her little dog was a Scotty. His hair was the same color as hers and just as coarse. He also had a snippy attitude. The dog's name was Fluffy. I could not believe they named a little wiry-haired dog Fluffy.

Fluffy got out of the house one afternoon and came strutting right up to Grundy, who was tied on his line in the back yard. Fluffy growled and postured; Grundy looked bored. For several minutes, Grundy patiently let Fluffy carry on. Finally, Grundy ran out of patience. He lifted one big paw and plunked it right in the middle of Fluffy's back. He didn't growl or bite. He just stood there. Fluffy was pinned to the ground, unable to move. You've never heard such yelping and screeching.

Our neighbor came running out of her house. "He's killing my Fluffy! He's killing my Fluffy!"

When the adults finally got everything under control, Bill calmly told the lady, "Believe me, if he'd wanted to kill Fluffy, he would have."

Neighborly relations were a bit strained after that.

Grundy lived a good long life. When Teen and Bill moved into their own home, I was invited to visit often. Teen bought a female Shepherd she named Cindy and mated the two dogs. They had two litters of pups. After the last litter was born, Grundy reached the end of his life. He was ten years old. Teen and Bill kept one of the puppies and named him "Schaefer," which in German means "shepherd."

I have known and loved quite a few dogs since Grundy. However, that big, beautiful German Shepherd is the reason I am a dog lover today. Grundy taught me life lessons that became a part of me. He taught me the importance of gentleness, faithfulness, and unconditional love; and that sometimes, it is perfectly okay to just put your foot down.

Chapter 12
Oatmeal and Other Goodies

M y foster mother, Bessie, worked hard. She kept a clean house and we were always fed well. Maybe it wasn't our favorite food, but if was put in front of us, we were expected to eat it, like it or not.

Living with Bessie and her family, I quickly learned to my utter dismay that these people liked mashed potatoes and mashed turnips. They put both on their plate and then proceeded to mix them together. I liked mashed potatoes, but I had no use for the turnips. They were sour! However, there was no way of getting out of eating them. If I turned up my nose, or made a face, or said one word about not liking turnips, I received an extra generous spoonful as a reward for my rebellion. I kept my face expressionless as the bitter root was served. Then, I held my breath and got rid of the turnips as quickly as possible.

Bessie could be the best cook in the world. Her pot roast was to die for. Beef stew was an awesome treat. She was a genius with pie crust. She didn't even have a recipe. It was all kept in her head. I still compare every pastry crust I make with hers. In my mind, I have never quite measured up to her standard.

I would hang out in the kitchen watching her making holiday pies and she made a bunch of them. She would quickly roll the dough out until it far extended over the pie plate. Then she whacked off great chunks of it with a knife, placed them on a cookie sheet, brushed them with butter, and sprinkled it all with cinnamon and sugar. She popped these odd shaped pieces of pastry into the oven for a few minutes. All the children in the house hovered at the oven door, waiting for our first taste of this incredible delicacy. Then the artist would really go to work. In the twinkling of an eye, it seemed, she had a beautiful fluted edge on the pie. I never did figure out how she did it. I have spent many holidays practicing and trying to duplicate what I watched her do over and over. She did it with one hand! Just her thumb and index finger and a flick of the wrist and she had a beautiful, perfect pie crust.

Summertime was not fun for me. We planted a vegetable garden every year and although I hated pulling the weeds out there in the hot sun, I certainly enjoyed the fruits of our labors. My favorite summertime meal was fried tomatoes in milk gravy, corn on the cob—fresh from the garden—and watermelon for dessert. Fresh cucumbers with onions mixed with vinegar and mayonnaise was another favorite. We had green beans, carrots, squash, and tomatoes all from our own garden.

There were times, however, that the food Bessie prepared was less than spectacular. In the summer, we had cereal and cold milk for breakfast. In the winter, we usually had two choices: one was shredded wheat with hot milk and the other was oatmeal. We all know hot milk disintegrates crisp shredded wheat. Enough said.

Oatmeal, on the other hand, was something else entirely. Bessie had a special pan she reserved for oatmeal. Obviously, it was very old. It was banged up and battered. The bottom was no longer flat but rounded and pockmarked. It wobbled when someone would set on the stove. I am sure that the very first batch of oatmeal cooked in that pan when it was new must have been burnt. That burnt taste remained for all the years the pan was used. Bessie never considered using any other utensil for cooking oatmeal. I hated oatmeal. I didn't know it was not supposed to taste burnt. I often fantasized about trashing that pan.

I will never forget one terribly hot summer evening when I asked what we were having for dinner.

"Split Pea Soup," Bessie said.

I groaned inwardly. Not only was it not one of my favorites but I couldn't imagine why she picked the hottest day of the year to make soup for dinner. While I wasn't happy about it, as I've said, the children in the home came to the table and ate what was put in front of us. We dared not complain or we would be punished or just receive more of the food we didn't like. This time, though, rebellion won out over good sense. I simply made up my mind that I would not eat that soup if I had to go hungry until the next day.

Bessie caught on pretty quickly. "You will sit at that table until you eat every bit of that soup."

I don't care if I have to stay here until midnight; I am not going to eat this soup.

Dinner was always at 5:30 p.m. and it wasn't long until everyone else had finished eating and left the table. I was sitting there alone, stubbornly refusing to eat. Time dragged on. It was 6:00 and then 6:30.

Tick, tick, tick.

The dining room clock reminded me of each minute that passed. I remember looking at the clock when it was 7:25. I didn't care. I intended to spend the night in that dining room. "But wait, what was that I just heard? Was that a distant rumble of thunder?" My fear of thunderstorms was far greater than my fear of Bessie. I quickly decided I was not going to win this battle. The one thing I did not want was to be sitting alone at this huge dining room table during a storm. *Oh well, I guess I have to eat this stuff.* By this time, the soup was cold and thick with a skin on top. I knew I would have to down it rather quickly too because of the threatening storm. By now it was 7:45 or thereabouts.

I gathered my courage, made a face, and took a deep breath. I stuffed a large spoonful of this awful green stuff in my mouth. At that split second, there was a wild flash of lightning and a deafening clap of thunder that seemed as if it were right on top of me. I leaped out of my chair, choking on the cold soup. I made a beeline for the bathroom. I only made it halfway up the steps before losing everything I'd eaten all day, making an awful mess. I was sure I was about to receive the beating of my life.

I will never know why, but Bessie just glared at me, and in a very disapproving voice, told me to go get ready for bed. I was stunned. I scurried up the steps and into my bedroom as she began the job of cleaning up the mess I'd made. As I closed my bedroom door, I have to admit there was a certain smug self-satisfaction in my mind. I had won by default! I will even admit to a smile and a "So there!" Under my breath, of course.

Chapter 13
The Birds and the Bees

I was ten years old and school was over for the year. It was early summer, and the weather was good and warm, although not quite the extreme heat and humidity that would come later. My friends and I had a fierce game of tag going on when I heard my foster mother calling me to come inside. I was really irritated because she always seemed to call me just when I was having fun. I knew better than to delay or to indicate in any way how annoyed I was. When she called like that, it meant now! Sighing at the interruption, I called to my friends and told them I'd be back later.

Running into the kitchen all hot and sweaty, I grabbed a quick drink of water before I presented myself at the "throne" (that's what I called her chair by the kitchen table). Bessie said she had something important to talk to me about. Of course, all I could think was, *What have I done now?* She took a long time before she spoke. I assumed it must be really bad because it seemed difficult for her to talk about. I quickly reviewed in my mind the events of the last few days. I could not think of anything I'd said or done that would get me into trouble, but Bessie's idea of trouble was always far different than mine.

Finally, she spoke. "If you ever go to the bathroom and see blood in your panties, come and tell me right away."

I stood there, not sure what she expected of me.

After a long, uncomfortable silence, she finally continued. "That's all, you can go on out and play now."

I had no idea what she was talking about and I was only too glad to get out of the house. Her remark confused me and left me questioning what in the world she could possibly have meant, but I was in a hurry to get back to the game. I couldn't be bothered worrying about it now.

Later though, when I was alone, I mulled over what she had said. It only confused me more. For the next two years, each bathroom visit was done in abject fear. I couldn't bring myself to ask her what she'd meant, and I had no one else to ask. Her statement became a neon sign in my brain: "If you ever . . ." It never occurred to me to ask my mother.

When I was twelve, it finally happened. I went running downstairs to tell my foster mother. My heart was pounding. I knew I must have some terrible disease. I was sure I was going to die. I ran into the kitchen where she was sitting and blurted it out.

Her reaction stunned me. She calmly turned, picked up her purse, and took out some money. "Here, take this, go to the grocery store, and this is what you get." She wrote down some things and sent me off to the store.

I crept toward the store with my mind in a whirl. I had no idea what was happening. How could she be so calm and not even care that I could be dying?

I had to ask a clerk at the store for the products I had on my list. She showed me where they were. I made the purchase and took my time walking home. Reporting in at the "throne," I was told to go upstairs to the bathroom and put them on. Bessie gave no explanation and did not offer to show me how to use the products. I simply went upstairs, read the instructions, and did what they said. I still had no idea what was happening to me. No one told me I was growing up and it was perfectly normal and healthy.

Chapter 14
Christmas Song

WHEN I WAS IN FIFTH grade, my mother scheduled a visit for two weeks or so before the Christmas holiday. This surprised me in a way because usually, her visits came after Christmas. However, the only thing that was important to me was that I would be spending the entire day with my mother.

It didn't matter what we did, we always had a great time when we were together. That afternoon, we were at Davis' Drug Store on Winona Avenue having a fountain drink.

"Do you know the song, 'Have Yourself a Merry Little Christmas?'" Mother asked.

"I know I've heard Judy Garland sing it, but I don't really know it."

Her voice became softer as she quoted the lyrics.

She took me through the song verse by verse. It is filled with hope and optimism.

"I know things are hard just now," she said. "I hate that we have to be separated and we don't get to see one another very often. I know you miss your brother. There is nothing I wish for more than for us—you, Billy, and me—to be together. Someday, I am sure that will happen, but until then, I want you to be brave and happy. Things will get better. In the meantime, I want you to have a very Merry Christmas." She went on to say, "From now on, whenever you hear this song, I want you to think of me and your brother and smile. This will be our special song and whenever I hear it, I will be thinking of you and Billy and I'll be smiling, too."

I remember having a feeling that there was more that my mother wanted to say, something she just could not express. I waited, but she said nothing more.

Too soon, the day was ending, and it was time for Mother to start the long commute back to the city. I stood, waving to her as the bus pulled away, and just as she'd told me, from then on, when I heard that song, I thought of her. To this day, whenever I hear that song, I think of her and that special day we had together, and I smile.

Christmas came and went as did New Year's. School started again, and I was so glad. At least I could be away from the house most of the day.

One day in early January, I came home from school and as I opened the front door, I was greeted with an angry tirade from my foster mother. This time, at least, it was not directed at me. She held a letter in her hand. Obviously, this letter was not good news. She was going on and on about my mother and how selfish and thoughtless she was.

I was confused. At first, I was afraid something had happened to my mother. Then I realized that Mother had done something that made Bessie really angry.

She finally blurted out the problem. "She's in California! California!"

I didn't understand. "Who's in California?"

"Your mother!" she screamed at me.

I was stunned. *That can't be right. Mother lives in Philadelphia.*

Then I thought that maybe Mother was in California visiting someone. But no, as Bessie continued, it became clear that Mother had moved to California with my Aunt Emma, Uncle Bill, and Cousin Joan. Not only that, but she'd already been there a month or so. Mother must have known she was going to California when she came to visit that last time.

Bessie went on and on about what a terrible and rotten person my mother was. As she continued to berate her, I knew she was also blaming me because I was sure Bessie hated my mother. I was just as certain she hated me, too. I felt sick and abandoned. When would I ever see my mother again? What about Billy? Where was he? Did he go with her? With no more visits to look forward to, I was stuck forever with this mean, angry foster mother. Now I had no one on my side. Again, I knew despair.

Chapter 15
Avoiding Bill

The weather turned beautiful and warm. Spring was in the air. I was nearing the end of sixth grade, looking forward to junior high at Glen-Nor High School. Seventh through ninth grades were considered junior high. Senior high school was tenth through twelfth grades. However, all grades were housed in the same building.

Teen's husband, Bill, was around the house more than I'd ever noticed before. He had always been just one of the adults I treated with respect because I had to, but we had no personal relationship. Now he began to strike up conversations with me. He asked about school and what I liked to do, things like that. I couldn't say why but this new friendliness made me uncomfortable. He even stopped to talk when I was outside with my friends. It seemed that I was always running into him. However, I was too busy being a kid with a whole summer ahead of her to be aware of any danger.

There came a day, though, when I was home alone. I was running downstairs on my way outside. Bill startled me. As I made the turn onto the lower landing, he was standing at the bottom of the stairs, blocking my way. I hadn't heard him come in. He should have been at work. I told him Bessie wasn't home and tried to skirt around him to continue my way outside. He said he knew that. Bill was a very big man and quite intimidating. He made no move to let me pass.

"You're really growing up," he said. "You've changed a lot." His voice was different. It got soft and husky. I'd never heard him talk like that. Suddenly I was very frightened.

Bill's trips to the house became even more frequent and he began to pursue me. He knew when I would be home alone. At first, it was just talking and stroking my arm or putting his arm around my shoulders. Things progressed from there to touching me and then forcing me to touch him. He was big and strong. If I resisted, he'd get angry. That really frightened me. I believed if I didn't do what he wanted, that he would beat me. I had no idea I was being sexually abused. I didn't know there was such a thing. I'd been taught to do what adults told me to do without argument or questioning. For the next three months, I was pursued and sexually abused by my foster sister's husband. I felt like a rabbit trying to get away from a fox. I was so frightened I would hide in a closet when Bill came around. How did he always know when I would be home alone?

Being at home alone became my biggest fear. I made sure to lock the doors, but Bill had a key. I was constantly checking the front of the house, the back of the house, and all the windows. I had to be certain he was not lurking around before I would venture out. My life became one of torment. Even though I was terribly naïve, instinctively I knew that what was going on was wrong. I hated the sight of him. He literally made me sick to my stomach.

One morning, he got me down on the floor in the dining room and tried to rape me. I was too small for him and he left feeling very frustrated and angry. I went upstairs and took a bath. I didn't see Bill for few days after that. It was a relief.

Bessie sent me to the grocery store one afternoon. The Acme, as it was called, stood on a corner. Huge plate glass windows lined the front and side of the building. From inside the store, you could see the corner and both intersecting streets easily. Waiting in the checkout line, I suddenly spotted Bill standing on the side of the store where I would be walking home. I knew why he was there. I began to tremble. I knew he was angry at me and the thought of what he might do frightened me. He would expect to continue where he'd left off a few days before. Underneath my fear, however, a little spark of anger began to flare.

A plan formed in my mind as I paid the cashier. Instead of turning left out of the store and going down Winona Avenue, I could turn right onto Chester Pike. This would be the long way home. I knew if I was late, I was in for it at home. Spurred on by fear and anger, I reasoned, *If I'm lucky, Bill will not see me.*

There was great risk in my plan. First of all, Bill might see me going the other way and he could easily run me down. But, there was an even greater risk. The ironclad rule at home was, "Go directly to the store, get what is on the list, and come directly home." Bessie timed me and if I took longer than she thought I should, I was in big trouble. The route I was taking was much longer than my usual way home. By this time, I couldn't have told you if I was more frightened of Bessie or Bill. I only knew that I was terribly frightened. There was no way this could turn out well. I slipped out the door and turned right, down Chester Pike toward St. Gabriel's Catholic Church.

One of the many rules was to always respect the church property and not be taking shortcuts through it, but I was desperate. By the time I reached St. Gabe's, as we called it, I was running full tilt. I turned into the church property, staying near the edge of the campus. Being as inconspicuous as possible was my plan. I didn't want one of the priests to yell at me. Quickly and quietly, I managed to get through the church property without getting caught. Taking this way took me three blocks farther than I would normally have to go. It brought me to the street in back of our house so that I had to come into our back yard and through the back door. As I ran, desperate to get home in time, a feeling of triumph began to surface. I had fooled Bill and he had not caught me! I had won! I laughed as I ran.

Banging through the back door, I was still laughing triumphantly, although, I was out of breath and sweating. Bessie and Teen were seated at the kitchen table, talking over a glass of iced tea. They both looked surprised because I usually came in the front door. I'm sure they wondered why I was in such a state. I placed the groceries on the table and bent over to catch my breath. When I could talk, I started to laugh again. Without thinking, I blurted out, "Well, I fooled Bill that time. He was waiting for me at The Acme, but I turned the other way and came home through St. Gabe's. He never even saw me!"

The look that passed between mother and daughter was electric. At that moment, something really significant was communicated without a single word. Yet they both understood clearly. I recognized that, but I did not understand what it was. Neither said a word. Bessie simply told me to put the groceries away and go out and play. So, I did. I could not believe I wasn't in trouble for taking the long way home. I went to search for my friends.

Later, as I headed downstairs for dinner, I passed Teen and Bill's room. I could hear muffled voices. I couldn't understand the words, but I could tell there was something wrong. Teen was obviously really angry. I knew better than to try to listen, so I hurried on downstairs.

A great tension filled the room at dinner that night. You could say there was an elephant in the room. Little conversation passed between the adults. What conversation there was sounded strained and awkward. I still didn't understand what had happened, but somehow, I knew I was at the center of all the tension. I was certain I had done something wrong. I kept my head down and ate my dinner in silence.

That day ended the sexual encounters. Bill never touched me again and I was never in a room alone with him. As far as I can remember, we never had a one-on-one conversation again. Shortly thereafter, Teen and Bill moved into their own place.

What has always puzzled me is that the matter was never spoken of again. I was so naïve that I didn't even know what had happened to me. No one ever bothered to explain it to me either. I felt guilty. There was no reason for me to feel that way. I hadn't done anything wrong. Yet somehow, it was my fault. I felt dirty and used. My thoughts and feelings were all jumbled up and confused. I could not understand why I should feel guilty. I was afraid to ask my foster mother or Teen. It seemed best to just let the subject drop.

The whole experience reminds me of someone putting his or her hand in a bucket of water and stirring the water into a frenzy. Once that person removes his or her hand, the water returns to being still and calm. No one ever asked if I'd been hurt or if I was all right. Life simply continued on as if nothing had happened.

I would have said that some of the fear eventually subsided, but I know now that I just buried it. I returned to school and never said a word to anyone about my horrible summer.

It wasn't until eighth-grade health class, two years later, that I learned what sex was and what had happened to me. It was many more years before I understood that what I'd experienced was sexual abuse.

A Special Note

I strongly resisted writing the preceding. I wanted those memories to remain buried forever, never to be looked at again.

The Lord's hand was on me for a long time, urging me to sit down and write this part. I reserved Sunday nights for writing. My husband was bowling, and I had some time to myself when I wrote this chapter. The Thursday before I wrote this part of the story, I felt the Lord impressing on me that *this* Sunday was the day. He let me know we had an "appointment."

"Lord, I don't want to do this."

As clearly as if He were in the room with me, I heard Him say, "I know." That was all.

I didn't even want to look at this chapter in my life and dredge it all up again. However, I knew that my Father was expecting me to obey Him.

A Christian radio station was on while I was working on this. As I finished writing this chapter, the station played one of my favorite songs. "Wayfaring Stranger" struck a chord in my heart years before I understood what the song meant. As a child, this song stirred something in me. I have sung the song many times. Now, at this moment, it caught my attention. It is not a song that is played often on the radio. I paused and went into the bedroom where the radio is and found myself praying the lyrics of the song out loud.

I lifted my hands to the Lord when I sang. "I'm goin' there to see my Jesus, I'm goin' there, no more to roam. I'm just a-goin' over Jordan. I'm just a goin' over Home."

His presence and sweet peace wrapped itself around me. I thanked the Lord for what I believe to be a confirmation that I had done well.

I started to leave the room and go back to the computer when an amazing thing happened. The song ended and immediately, the station played another version of it. How many times does a radio station play two versions of the same song back to back? *This was a God thing!* Now I was down on my knees and again I "prayed" the song. Tears streamed down my face as I felt His very presence in the room with me. God was telling me He was pleased.

Chapter 16
Moving On

I turned thirteen that October. I had just come through the worst time of my life. I'd been sexually abused all summer. After that was over, I contracted shingles. To this day, I can remember the pain and itching associated with that condition. The rash was all around my waist in about a three-inch swath. I can remember the awful cold when the calamine lotion touched my skin. I shivered and tried to pull away. Evidently, this was the only treatment available at the time. If I tried to rub or scratch the itch, the pain was terrible—burning and sharp at the same time. The scabs were the worst. They caught on my clothes, causing more pain. My skin felt hot and feverish.

"It isn't good that the rash is around your waist," my foster mother said. "If it ever gets all the way around to your backbone, you'll die."

How could anyone be so cruel to tell a kid an old wives tale like that? I was downright panicked. I'd stand in front of the mirror every day, trying to twist around to see how close the rash was to my backbone, which only caused more pain.

No one in the family ever talked about it but I am certain the events of that awful summer were the reason Teen and Bill moved into their own home. My foster brother, Ed, joined the Army, and Bessie and I were the only ones left at home. Bessie got a job as a practical nurse in a nursing home. Her shift was 11:00 p.m. until 7:00 a.m. I was usually home by the time she had to leave for work and I would just be getting ready for school in the morning when she arrived home. That part of the new arrangement suited me just fine.

However, Teen and Bill's leaving brought a whole new set of problems for me. Although I was relieved that Bill was gone, I was often alone in the house. I hated that. As long as I could remember, I had always been afraid of the dark. Being alone in that big, drafty house that creaked and groaned was terrifying. I jumped at every noise and I was up several times during the night, checking to make sure doors were locked and there was no one around. I dared not go down into the cellar or up into the attic. I couldn't bring myself to do that. Finally, I would force myself to go to bed. After several hours of lying awake, sleep would finally come.

Some things did change for the better. Teen and I became closer. I suspect that this was not the first time that Bill had been involved in some kind of sexual episode. She seemed to appoint herself my special protector and friend. She asked me to help her with some housecleaning and she paid me for it, too. Bill was never in the home while I was there. In fact, as I thought about it, I seldom saw him. I have often wondered if the episode caused them to separate.

For the first time, I was earning my own spending money. Teen bought me a used bicycle. I was twelve years old and this was my first bike. What a joy to ride away from the house to freedom. I rode my bike to the store, and all over Norwood and Glenolden. Sometimes, I just visited my friends. And other times, I rode and rode because it felt so good to be free.

Teen introduced me to a doctor and his family. They had five children and needed a babysitter, so they hired me at fifty cents an hour. This was just another opportunity for me to get away from the house. I babysat for them for several years every afternoon and sometimes on Friday or Saturday nights.

Mother returned from California around this time. Things had not worked out the way she thought they would. She told me that Aunt Emma had painted such a rosy picture of beautiful California that she agreed to try it.

"You'll be able to get a good job out there and then you can send for the kids," Aunt Emma told her.

But Mother hated California.

The Christmas following that awful summer, Teen bought me a cheap, used Harmony guitar. In so doing, she opened a door to a whole new wonderful world for me—the world of music. She didn't have a lot of money and I so appreciated that gift. I escaped to my room and spent hours practicing. I was self-taught because we didn't have money for lessons.

One afternoon, I came downstairs after practicing for a couple of hours. Bessie shocked me with what I think was a compliment.

"You know, when you're up there practicing, it sounds just like an old-time player piano," Bessie said. She never offered compliments, but I chose to look at this remark as her way of trying to encourage me.

Chapter 17
The Blue Sky Riders

That guitar changed my life. It took me places I could have never imagined. A friend from school, Jerry Borton, was super smart, studious, and quiet. He was just an all-around nice guy. He was a "geek" before such a word even existed. Jerry must have been very unhappy in public school where he was often teased and taunted. His parents enrolled him in a private school in Philadelphia. He was also a talented musician, especially on the steel guitar.

Jerry telephoned me one day to tell me he was starting a hillbilly band. He invited me to play guitar and sing with him. That type of music wasn't even dignified with the title of "country" back then. I was surprised and thrilled that he would even consider asking me to join his band. Of course, I said yes.

Being invited to be part of this little band was one of the most exciting things that ever happened to me. I was convinced I didn't have many friends. I didn't feel as if I fit in anywhere. Over the years, I have learned that I was really mistaken. Many of my classmates are still my friends. However, in those junior high and high school years, I did not believe I belonged anywhere or to anyone.

Jerry's parents sponsored our band. Mrs. Borton worked with the American Red Cross and through her connections, she found us places to perform. Mr. Borton was our driver, tech advisor, operations manager, equipment hauler, and "roadie." They had a long, low-slung car; I believe it was a Hudson. We jammed all the instruments and equipment into the trunk. Then we slid the bass fiddle into the car with the neck extending to the front between the driver and the passenger seat. The stand (or foot, if you will) rested on the back shelf of the rear window. The body of the bass fiddle was suspended over the back seat.

Mr. Borton drove while Mrs. Borton was in the passenger seat. Jerry and I squeezed into the back seat, one on either side of the bass. We had no chance of seeing anything out the back window. It must have been a funny sight.

Jerry's sister, Patsy, was a petite blonde with sparkling white teeth. I will always remember that beautiful smile. The bass was Patsy's instrument. Dwarfed by that huge bass fiddle, she could make that thing talk.

Jerry played a fine steel guitar. Like me, he had taught himself. Unlike me, he was a natural talent. At the time, I listened to nothing but hillbilly music. There were a number of professional steel guitar players I admired. As young as Jerry was, I truly believe he was as good as any of them. He made it look easy.

I played rhythm guitar and sang. We had a couple of accordion players over the time we were together. Eddie Andrews was one and when Eddie had to leave us, Rudy Mager took over the accordion duties. We called ourselves The Blue Sky Riders.

Mr. Borton made a huge round sign with our logo on it and Jerry attached it to his steel guitar stand when we played.

I loved entertaining. Stage fright was not a problem for me. In some way, I think being on stage satisfied some need in me for attention. Veterans hospitals were my favorite places to entertain. I had never seen anything like the pain and suffering that I saw there. These men had come back from the Korean War with all kinds of injuries. Many of them faced long bouts of recovery and therapy. They were away from their families and lonely. We provided a diversion for them that they so appreciated. We would greet them after our performance. They always expressed gratitude for the music and for our taking the time to come and play for them. As for us, we were thrilled to have the opportunity to play our music. After all, we were going to be big music stars someday.

Chapter 18
The Choice

Our little town boasted a neighborhood theater, complete with a gaudy marquee out front that boldly proclaimed the current feature and some of the coming attractions. It was my special place to escape. Every Saturday, I attended a matinee for eighteen cents. For that tiny admission price, there was a full-length feature film, several cartoons, and a newsreel. Quite often, we were treated to a double feature! Those were great days. I entered that dark cavern of delight at around 12:30 in the afternoon and did not come out until 5:00 or 5:30 pm. The sun was disappearing and soon it would be dark and cold. I felt as if I'd been far away in a time machine and had just returned to earth. The best part was I'd escaped my life for those few precious hours.

One Saturday, my mother came to visit, and we went to the matinee together. The theater was just a short walk from my house. We walked together hand in hand, talking and laughing. We had such a good time that afternoon. I was excited to spend all this time with her. I knew that it would be late that night when she finally got home, and I was so grateful. She would be tired on Sunday, her only day off from work.

As we came out of the theater and started home, Mother's conversation turned serious. Although she didn't mention the sexual abuse, I was sure she knew about it. We talked about how unhappy I was and the constant verbal abuse and fear. Suddenly she asked me if I'd like to come live with her. My heart leaped for joy. This very thing had been the desire of my heart for years! My mother wanted me! I could be with her and my brother. I wanted to laugh and dance and yell, "Yes! Yes! Yes!" How could I not want to live with her?

"But wait!" Questions began to flood my mind. What about the band? What about school? What about my friends? I'd have to start all over again. I'd heard there were cops patrolling every floor in the Philadelphia schools. The big city scared me. Mother's apartment was small. I wondered how three of us would manage in such a small place. Now I was no longer so sure of my answer. I quietly asked her if I could have some time to think it over. She told me there was no rush and I could take all the time I needed.

I struggled with this question for a long time. On the one hand, I would be with my mother and my brother whom I missed terribly. I could escape the "prison" where I lived. That's how I thought of my home; I was free only when I was away from the house.

I knew my foster mother would not miss me. It would make no difference to her if I left. On the other hand, I faced an uprooting of everything that was familiar to me.

I went to rehearsal and thought about how much I would miss Mr. and Mrs. Borton, and Jerry and Patsy. The Borton family had become very dear to me. With them, I knew I was accepted and welcome. I would miss playing and singing for the guys at the veterans hospitals. They were always so nice and appreciated the time we spent with them.

At school, I'd say a cheery hello to our band director, Mr. O'Neill, and think to myself, "There can't be another teacher like him anywhere." I looked up to him. He treated me like a real person.

Every school day, I walked to my friend Vonnie's house, about five minutes from mine. We continued on to school together, chatting and laughing all the way. I would miss her. Barbara Sue was another dear friend I would miss.

When my foster mother allowed it, I went to my friend, Judie's, house on Saturdays. Her mom and dad treated me like one of the family. Her dad was so handsome, and I think I had a kind of crush on him. He was funny, too. Judie's mom had a collection of milk glass chickens. Right before I went home, amidst much giggling, Judie and I turned the chickens around so their tail feathers would be facing out. We pretended that her mom had no idea what we were doing. She would laugh and say, "Well, I know Carole's been here today."

Bessie gave me a stern warning to be home no later than 6:00 p.m. I always waited until the last possible minute to leave Judie's house. Then I pedaled my bike as fast as my legs could go, desperately praying, "Dear God, please help me get home on time."

How could I just say goodbye to all of these friends? Yet, my heart yearned to be with my mother and brother.

I believed I had no one in whom I could confide or ask for advice. Actually, there were quite a few adults I could have turned to for counsel. Mr. O'Neill was one. However, I did not trust adults. It was many weeks before I came to a decision and when I did, it broke my heart.

The next time my mother came to visit, I told her that I had decided to stay where I was. Looking into her eyes, I could see the pain and disappointment. She didn't cry, and she didn't question my decision, but I knew I had hurt her deeply. For many years, I was not able to forgive myself. Of all the people in my life, my mother was the one person I never wanted to hurt. She'd had enough pain. For months, I reviewed my decision in my mind over and over again. I felt so guilty for hurting this woman I loved. Mother assured me that she accepted my decision. She made sure I knew I could change my mind anytime.

As time went on, everyday life kind of got in the way. Gradually I accepted the reality of the decision I'd made. I went on with school and my music. I made new friends and had new experiences. Deep in my heart though was the knowledge that I had rejected the one person I loved the most.

Life was not any happier for me after I decided to stay in my foster home. However, I noticed subtle changes. I don't know if it had anything to do with my being victimized by Teen's husband, but it seemed as if I didn't get in trouble as often. Bessie began treating me as an older child, rather than a little kid. During the next few years, we even sat at the kitchen table and actually talked on occasion. She was supportive of my activities with The Blue Sky Riders. She encouraged me to keep it up, although she did not come to any of my performances. She was never in attendance at any of my school programs either. But to my surprise, she began to let me go out on my own more often. I either rode with the Bortons or other families or simply walked to school when there was something going on.

My books and my radio became my very best friends. A good book would pull me in and I simply escaped into the world the author had created. I can't begin to count the number of times I was yelled at because I got so lost in a book. I simply did not hear my foster mother calling me. She'd suddenly be standing over me berating me, telling me how disrespectful and stupid I was. I was always surprised to see her there.

"Escape" was my watchword. I crowded as much as I could into my schedule. If there was an opportunity to be involved in something at school, I volunteered. I made arrangements to spend Saturdays at a friend's house. Yet, no matter how busy I was or how much fun I was having, there was always the echo of those words that I knew had hurt my mother deeply.

School was my refuge. At school, I could be myself. Teachers and friends treated me with respect and affection. I lived two separate lives. When I walked out the front door, I was a different person than I was behind that door. Inside that house, I was fearful and nervous. I tried hard to be compliant and subservient. I became quite the little actress. In my mind, I referred to myself as "The Great Pretender." Away from home, I was free to be whomever I wanted to be. School was a safe haven and I dreaded being home. Walking home from school, my footsteps slowed as I neared the house. I was constantly fearful that I would do or say something that would get me in trouble. As I placed my hand on the doorknob, I couldn't help but think, *Well, I wonder what I am in trouble for today?* Most of the time, my expectations were correct. Usually, Bessie was angry about something and I was most often the cause.

Chapter 19
Gigs

On Sundays during the summer, The Blue Sky Riders traveled to parks where there were music festivals. These were all-day affairs with several bands performing. I loved these Sundays. Not only was I doing what I loved; performing with my friends, but I got a full day of listening to others play my favorite music. Some of the guys played the bars on Friday and Saturday nights and then came to the parks on Sunday. We met some interesting characters.

In the summer of 1953, we played Steel Pier in Atlantic City. Steel Pier was an entertainment extravaganza and was famous the world over. This was the home of the famous Diving Horses. These horses would enter the arena through a steep ramp. Urged to the top of the ramp by a beautifully dressed young rider, the animal would pause dramatically at the edge and suddenly leap off the ramp into a huge pool. It was the most exciting thing I'd ever seen!

Several theaters were featured on Steel Pier, as well as exhibits and an arcade. A person could spend hours, perhaps even days exploring all of it. One of the theaters on Steel Pier was the youth theater. Here, young singers, dancers, and performers of all types had an opportunity to show off their talent. We felt like we'd hit the big time.

We did four shows a day in the Tony Grant Youth Theater. Between shows, we could do whatever we chose, as long as we were back in time to get ready for the next show. It was a grueling schedule, but we hardly noticed; we were running on pure adrenalin. What a week that was. I took in as much of Steel Pier as possible. For our performances, we dressed in our western finery, complete with hats and boots. I even had a black satin skirt with white fringe on the hem and a black and white western shirt which I'd paid for with my babysitting money. We were duded up!

One evening, Mr. Tony Grant, the director of the youth theater, took the whole cast to an Italian restaurant to celebrate a successful week. I hadn't been to many restaurants. In fact, I can only remember one, the Norwood Restaurant. My mother sometimes took me to lunch there. This Italian place was grand; elegant, quiet, and beautiful. Of course, I ordered spaghetti and meatballs. What else would you choose? Then we finished it up with spumoni. I'd never tasted spumoni. To this day, I don't feel like I've really had an Italian dinner unless it is topped off with that delectable treat.

We appeared on television as part of the *Paul Whiteman Show* in July of 1954. Paul Whiteman was a very well-known big band leader. It was an honor for us to take second place.

For a time, we had our own fifteen-minute live radio show. It was on a little local station that boasted just two tiny studios. We were scheduled back to back with Bill Haley and the Comets! Of course, that was before, "Rock Around the Clock." I had no idea who Bill Haley was. From what I understood, his band was simply playing the local bars and clubs around suburban Philadelphia, hoping to get a break.

This radio station was so small that it was downright comical as we tried to get out of the studio so Bill Haley and his group could get into it during a news break. Believe me, it was tight quarters trying to get equipment and people in and out of that little entryway. Even once we were set up inside the studio, we could barely move. It was hard to imagine there was a real audience listening as we stood in front of those big microphones. My dreams of stardom took off. After all, here I was on the radio! I must be well on my way to stardom. I was so naïve.

I played with The Blue Sky Riders from 1951 to 1956. It was the adventure of my young life. Everything was exciting. Arriving home after a performance was a letdown. I wanted my whole life to be singing, performing, and being part of the world of music. This was a world of joy and I wanted it to never end. We played talent shows, banquets, parties, churches, rescue missions, and anywhere else someone would give us an opportunity to entertain.

The most meaningful part of all this to me wasn't the rehearsing or the performing, the applause, or traveling all over the area. The Bortons themselves were the most important. They were a real family. I didn't have much experience with real families. They loved, laughed, and even argued some. And they included me in it all, making me part the family. This was a very special gift.

I pretended that Mr. and Mrs. Borton were the parents I didn't have. Jerry and Patsy were my brother and sister. I was an expert pretender. I'd had lots of practice. When things got tough, my imagination took over. I became a different person in a different world. Finally, I belonged to a real family. I am so grateful to have had the privilege of being one of the Bortons kids. I wish I'd been able to express to them how very much they meant to me.

Chapter 20
The Magic Garden of Music

My experiences playing and singing with The Blue Sky Riders stood me in good stead when I went to high school. I became a bit more outgoing than I'd been in elementary school and junior high. I still had no self-confidence or any illusion that I fit in anywhere, though.

I worked up the courage to audition for my high school variety show and I made it. "Y'all Come" was my big number. I played some guitar with the swing band and did some ensemble work. Glee club was my first experience with choral music and I've seldom been out of a choir since then.

Marlon O'Neill was the band and music director. All the kids loved him and would have done anything for him. He was tough, and he knew exactly what he wanted out of his musicians and he demanded it. He wore shoes with hard soles and he pounded out the timing on the floor in the gym with his foot. A shock of reddish blond hair was always falling in his eyes and he'd brush it back with his hand and yell, "Let's try that one again!" We loved him and feared him at the same time. He was the most handsome man I'd ever known and the nicest.

One afternoon in my sophomore year, I was walking down the hall between classes and I met Mr. O'Neill coming the other way.

"We are taking a field trip to the Academy of Music in Philadelphia to see the Philadelphia Orchestra," he said. "I thought maybe you'd like to go."

I remember looking at him like he was from outer space. He knew hillbilly music was the only thing I listened to and I thought he'd lost his mind. Me, go to a classical concert? That was practically blasphemy! I hesitantly told him I didn't think I'd like to do that.

He shrugged. "Oh, well, that's ok. You would get out of a full day's worth of classes, though."

Whoa, a day's worth of freedom from school work. That was an offer too hard to resist. I reconsidered quickly and told him I would go.

A field trip was a rare treat. We rode in a huge bus all the way to the city. We carried our lunches in paper sacks and had a picnic on the grounds near the Academy of Music. Then we entered a beautiful building that smelled old and musty. An elevator took us up several stories, but from there we had to walk up several more flights of stairs to the "peanut gallery." I remember thinking as I climbed, *I sure hope this is worth all this work.*

Finally, we reached the very top level of the auditorium. Completely out of breath, I looked down and saw the stage. It seemed so very far away. *What a waste of time this is going to be.* The concert hall was U-shaped, and we were led to the section closest to the stage. I landed a seat in the front row. I was still not sure I would be able to see much. A huge, leather-padded railing protected anyone from pitching off the balcony into the chasm below. Several of us placed our arms up on that railing. With our chins in our hands, we could survey the entire auditorium.

Suddenly, there was a stir as the orchestra members entered from backstage. They took their places on the stage. They were all dressed in black. The men wore tuxedos and the women wore long dresses. A sense of hushed anticipation filled the hall. Then, a smallish old man in a tuxedo entered and the whole place erupted in applause. His hair was white, and it looked to me like he hadn't bothered to comb it. This was the famous Eugene Ormandy. He took his place at the conductor's podium and tapped on the music stand to get the musicians' attention. Absolute silence fell over the entire auditorium and then the magic began.

I looked down into this chasm below me, the orchestra on my left and Mr. Ormandy to my right. The minute the music started, I froze. I don't think I moved through the entire concert. I had no idea there were such sounds in the world. I was fascinated by each instrument and the artist who played it. First, I looked at the musicians, and then at Mr. Ormandy. I must have resembled someone watching a tennis match, given the way my head bounced back and forth. Each musician concentrated completely and seemed to be enthralled with his or her work. Mr. Ormandy's face shone with what could only be called a look of pure love and pride as he guided the musicians expertly through the intricate music passages.

Sometimes the music started softly and built to a tremendous crescendo. There were times the entire piece was soft and gentle. Other times the entire orchestra played with an exuberance and intensity that filled the whole building with soaring melodies. I had entered a magic garden and the musical delights in this garden were endless.

Three hours later, it all came to an end. I found myself trying desperately to hang on to the lingering echoes. I wanted it to go on and on. Too quickly, our teachers ordered us to our feet and back to the bus. The spell was broken. The shuffling feet and silly giggles just ruined everything. However, I had been to a place of worship. The taste of that experience would never disappear from my heart and mind.

Riding the bus home that day, I began to think about how much I admired Mr. O'Neal and several other teachers. I was a sophomore and as my memory went back through my school years, it occurred to me that I had mostly good experiences with my teachers. Some of them I really loved. I decided that day that I wanted to become a teacher. When I arrived home, Bessie seemed to be in a good mood. I was excited to share my decision and so I told her that I wanted to go to college and become a teacher.

Bessie stopped what she was doing and turned to look at me. I remember exactly what she said. "Phfft, you're not college material. Who do you think you are? You're just a nobody." Then she went on to say, "Nice girls go to work in a bank or store and then get married and have babies." The conversation was over. She walked out of the room. I was crushed. For years afterward, I believed those words. They echoed in my heart and mind, causing me great pain.

Chapter 21
The Turning Point

Over and over throughout my walk with Jesus, other believers have stressed how important it is to write an account of your conversion. I didn't see the need. After all, I know how it happened. He knows, too. However, I've come to a place in my life where I see the value of a written account.

Whenever I considered writing about how I became a Christian, I knew exactly how I would tell it. I knew the exact date: December 23, 1953. It was in the evening service at Crum Lynn Baptist Church in Crum Lynn, Pennsylvania, a small suburb of Philadelphia. The pastor who was the messenger for a miraculous change in this young heart was Dan Bartkow. Dan was a tall, handsome fellow who had a beautiful singing voice. It was not only the words in his sermons that got my attention but when he sang about the love of Jesus, my heart wanted to sing along with him. The problem was, I didn't know this Person of whom he sang. I didn't know that I wanted or even needed a relationship with this Wonderful Savior he preached and sang about.

That December night, just before Christmas when I accepted Jesus into my heart as my personal Lord and Savior, was the culmination of six weeks of hearing, resisting, running away, and finally surrender. It was all captured in my heart and mind. I knew I could never forget it, but when I began to write about it, I came to a startling realization. Those six weeks were only a small part of the story. I learned that what I thought of as an isolated, yet wonderful experience in my life was not that at all. It was the end result of God's pursuing me for years. The Bible says, "The Lord is not slow in keeping his promise, as some understand slowness. Instead, he is patient with you, not wanting anyone to perish, but everyone to come to repentance" (2 Peter 3:9 NIV).

Back when I was that little girl who always seemed to be in trouble for one reason or another, I spent a good deal of time in my room. The foot board of my four-poster bed became my trusted steed on whose back I could pretend to be anyone and go anywhere I wanted. I was Dale Evans and yes, I was even a cowboy. I galloped my horse across the plains, roping calves and chasing bad guys. It was more fun being a boy than a girl because boys had it better than girls as far as my little eyes could see. The pretending only helped some of the time since I was convinced that I was a bad kid and I didn't know how to be any better.

The fact was, I was alone and there was no one who cared, except my mommy and she was not there. I did, however, have the Voice. This was not an audible sound but rather it was inside my head and my heart. Someone—I did not know His name—spoke to me. "It's all right, I'm here." I remember Him promising, "Someday, I will turn your upside-down life around and everything will be right-side up." The Voice was so real that sometimes I looked in my closet to see who was there. Then, I knelt down and looked under my bed, searching for who was speaking. Did I really hear the Voice? I knew I was the only one in my bedroom, but I was not alone. A comforting Presence was there in the room with me.

Bessie had a sister, Edith, who lived in West Philadelphia. Occasionally, we would make the long drive to visit her. On the way, in a town called, Upper Darby, there was a huge billboard that had been sponsored by a local church. In great big letters, it trumpeted: FOR THE WAGES OF SIN IS DEATH. I knew I was a sinner; my foster mother told me often how bad I was and that I would never amount to anything. That sign scared me and at the same time, I was drawn to read it every time we drove past it. I couldn't tear my eyes away. In smaller letters near the bottom of the billboard, there were some more words: "but the gift of God is eternal life through Jesus Christ Our Lord" (Romans 6:23). I didn't understand what I was reading but I felt fear and at the same time hope. There was a gift and that gift was somehow attainable through Jesus Christ. Those words haunted and disturbed me.

At that time, there was a young preacher on television and radio named Billy Graham. His deep southern accent sounded so strange to me and yet there was such sincerity and gentleness in his voice that I couldn't help but listen. He frightened me, too. He used those same words I'd seen on the billboard, but he explained them. I watched his rallies on TV and I listened to his radio broadcasts and still, I couldn't figure out how to receive this gift of eternal life.

It was all made clear to me when the Bortons invited me to a little Baptist Church in Crum Lynne, Pennsylvania. When Pat Borton asked me if I'd like to go to church with them the following Sunday, I was uncomfortable. I was fifteen years old and I had abandoned my earlier practice of going to church. I didn't want to go. The only reason I agreed this time was because I couldn't think of a good excuse.

That little church was unique. The sanctuary was in the shape of an "L." The pulpit was situated at the corner where the two lines of the" L" came together. People who were seated on both sides of the "L" could easily see. As the preacher, Dan Bartkow, spoke, I became more and more uncomfortable. It seemed to me that when he talked about sin, he was looking directly into my heart and speaking to me personally. He told us that if we lied, we were sinners. I had often lied to my foster mother just to try to stay out of trouble. My lying always seemed to make matters worse though. Dan said that if we harbored angry, bitter thoughts, we were sinners. I did not like what I was hearing because I didn't like myself. I felt so guilty. I became very angry and when I got home, I made up my mind that I would never go back to that church again.

The next week, just as before, I had no reasonable excuse when Pat asked if I would go to church again. The pattern was set and repeated each week for six weeks. I don't understand why, but Bessie did not object to me going to a Baptist church. Maybe it was because I was going with the Borton family. I never could figure out Bessie's reasoning for anything. She was probably glad to have me out of the house for a few hours.

I became secretly angry with these dear friends because I was certain they had talked to Dan about me. How could they tell him about my dark thoughts and my anger and fear and resentment? How dare they reveal my darkest secrets to this man I didn't even know? My guilt was so strong that I was convinced that everyone in the service could see through me and knew what a terrible person I was.

When I returned home after church one Sunday morning, as I entered the house, I slammed the front door as only a teenager can and loudly declared, "I will never go back to that church again!" For the next six Sundays, there I was, right where God wanted me. On that sixth Sunday, God brought understanding to my heart. I finally realized that I could do nothing to earn my salvation. It was a free gift that God had prepared for me by allowing His only Son to be the sacrifice for my sin, just because He loved me. It was almost too easy. All I had to do was say, "Yes, Lord Jesus, I accept your gift of salvation for me," but I wanted to declare it publicly.

I was scared out of my mind and very self-conscious, but I knew that I really wanted forgiveness and eternal life. Most of all, I needed peace in my life and Jesus promised that. I had to follow through and declare my faith in Jesus before the congregation. My face was burning, and I was warm all over, but I stood to my feet and confessed that I wanted to accept Jesus as my Lord and Savior. I would not presume to claim a vision, but I could see the Lord Jesus standing behind me with His hands on my shoulders. I have no memory of the words. I only know when He spoke, I recognized the Voice I had heard so many years ago as a little girl.

Chapter 22
Spreading My Wings

The next two years fell into a rhythm of school, music, friends, and being home alone. However, there were times when Bessie and I sat at the kitchen table and talked, much like she and Teen used to do. At those times, we seemed to connect, although the gulf between us never really disappeared. I longed to be a real part of her life. I still felt as though she would only allow me to get so close and no more. I desperately needed to belong to someone.

When Bessie and I sat and talked, sometimes I became too bold. One day, I asked, "What was life like in your family?" Immediately a door slammed closed and she completely shut down. Her wall was in place. Her reply was hard and cold. "Oh, you don't need to know about that stuff." She got up from the table, cleared the tea cups, and left the room.

What kind of pain must this woman have endured in her life? What dark secrets could cause that kind of bitterness?

A new dynamic entered our relationship. Bessie didn't spend a lot of time yelling at me and telling me how inept I was. The pressures she began to use were more subtle but still very strong. If I did not cooperate, she would threaten me with being confined to the house. Escaping that house was vital, so I usually did what she asked.

Dating opened a whole new round of conflict with Bessie. She made it very clear she did not trust me. She never spoke the words out loud. I just knew she disapproved of me and whomever I was dating. Puzzled and confused, I could not imagine what I had done to make her so suspicious of my every motive. Was she jealous because I was going places and had friends? I had no answers.

My first date came in my sophomore year of high school. Joe was a senior at St. James High School in Chester, Pennsylvania. I met him at a high school dance and we hit it off immediately. He was fun to be with and he drove his dad's car. A winning combination!

I loved Joe's family. They were warm and friendly and loud! His grandmother was from the "old country." The first thing she'd ask you when you entered the home was, "Didja eat yet?" Then she insisted you sit down and have a big serving of whatever wonderful delicacy she was creating that day. She would accept no excuses. She was going to take good care of you.

As I mentioned previously, my foster mother was prejudiced. Even people who met her criteria of being white, European, and Methodist, she spoke of as if they were evil. The Methodist part made no sense, because she never darkened the door of any church. It was so hypocritical.

Bessie's rules changed all the time. Although I had permission to go out with Joe, every time we had a date, Bessie made things difficult. In the hours before our date, she berated Joe for his looks, his religion, and his olive skin. Of course, she never said them in his presence. By the time he came to pick me up, I was angry and upset. It hurt me to hear her talk about my friend that way. I wished I could say something in his defense. I knew, however, that if I tried to argue, I wouldn't be permitted to go out with Joe at all.

Joe and I talked about all this at length. He was never resentful and didn't take it personally. He was kind and understanding. Our friendship was only strengthened by sharing our thoughts and feelings. He was always supportive and encouraging.

I had been dating Joe for about three months. Suddenly Bessie announced that I was no longer allowed to see him. She gave no reason, just the ultimatum. Things got really ugly. She yelled and hollered at me. She said if I wanted to be allowed outside the house at all, I would have to end the relationship.

I cried. "Why? What have we done that is so wrong?"

She gave me no answer except that I had to stop seeing him. I had no choice. I tried to think about all that had happened in the recent past. What brought on this sudden change? She gave no explanation and I was unable to change her mind.

Telling Joe that we could not date anymore was so very hard for me. We sat in his car and talked for a long time. I told him I was so sorry but I just couldn't fight my foster mother. We were really more like best friends than boyfriend and girlfriend. That night, we vowed that no one would destroy our friendship. Joe remained my friend for the rest of his life. He passed away while still in his thirties. But the night I broke the news to him, he was gracious and kind, as always. He introduced me to a friend of his, Jim, who also went to St. James. He was Irish and Catholic. Bessie was no more pleased with this young man than she had been with Joe.

I was so angry at Bessie. I no longer came to the kitchen table to talk. I had to treat her with respect, but I didn't speak to her any more than necessary. I thought of running away. I knew I could move in with my mother and brother, but that would mean giving up my friends, school, and the band. Those were all the good things I had in my life. I decided that I would not allow my foster mother to ruin my relationship with Jim. My back stiffened. I became more stubborn and determined.

Did Bessie sense a change in me? I don't know. Whatever the reason, Jim and I dated for two years, in spite of her opposition. I turned a deaf ear to the awful things Bessie would say about him. However, the problems and criticisms I faced dating Jim were no less than the ones with Joe. Bessie was just as vocal in her opinions as she'd ever been. Yet, over time, she seemed to take a liking to Jim. Sometimes, she even engaged him in conversation while I was getting ready for our date.

I dreamed about being Jim's wife. We were so comfortable together. I felt safe with him. He encouraged me and made me feel special. We went to dances, to the movies, and just had fun. We double dated with Joe and his new girlfriend, Betsy. Life was good. That is, except for when I had to go home.

The one difficulty Jim and I faced in our relationship was the difference in our religious beliefs. He was brought up in a structured, traditional, liturgical church background. The church was very important in his life. I had little knowledge of church. I had come to a simple faith in Jesus Christ. I had a personal relationship with Christ, my Savior. I was eagerly learning what the Bible said. My pastor and the Bortons encouraged me to read it on my own. Jim, on the other hand, said that the priest was the only one qualified to read and interpret the Bible. So, Jim and I did the only thing that made sense. We avoided the subject most of the time.

TIME PASSED QUICKLY. Graduation came. I took a job as a filing clerk at a bank in Philadelphia. All the while, I assumed Jim and I would marry. As our relationship turned more serious, we could no longer avoid the subject of our faith. We disagreed and that was the truth of it. I remember telling him not to try to convert me. A short time later, I received a large envelope of material about the Catholic church from the Knights of Columbus. There was so much written material, I thought, *I'll never be able to read all this*. Out of respect for Jim, I did read a good bit of it. However, I could not get past my anger at him for sending this to me when he had agreed to not try to convert me. I was livid.

I knew I could not give up my beliefs for Jim's. He had been raised in his faith and had a hard time understanding the simplicity of mine. For weeks, I struggled to find some way to hold on to this relationship and my newfound faith, at the same time. Over and over, I begged God to make a way. "Please Father, let me have You and Jim also." I received no answer. Finally, I had to admit in my heart there was no compromise. It was with great sadness that I told Jim we had to end our relationship. We parted as friends, but I was heartbroken, and it took me a long time to get over it. For many months, if I saw a green and white Oldsmobile like Jim's dad's car, my heart pounded in my chest. I kept hoping Jim would give in and see it my way. That never happened.

I didn't date for a long time. During this time, some of my friends at church invited me to a roller skating rink. I was hooked immediately. Skating became my passion and obsession. I bought an expensive pair of fancy roller skates and I was at the rink several times a week. The rink had a beautiful maple floor that was as smooth as glass, without any bumps or rough spots. A live organist provided the music. She played requests and the music always perfectly fit the particular skate dance we were doing. I met my friends there and we had a great time. We chased each other around the rink and challenged one another to race. I reveled in this new world I'd found. Everything I did became simply a way to pass the time until I could lace up my skates once again. That is, everything except church. I did not skate on Sundays.

I decided I needed my own vehicle. I bought a 1952 Chevy Sport Coupe with my own money. That car cost me a whopping $425.00. That was a lot of money in those days. I also paid for my driving lessons from a professional. I was so proud. I was grown up. For the first time in my life, I was in control. The faster I drove, the better I liked it. I was terrible. Drag racing gave me a thrill that was more exciting than anything I'd ever known. When I raced, I had power!

Chapter 23
One Wild Night

Roller skating changed my life. Why my foster mother didn't try to stop me from going to the rink, I never could understand. I was always on edge, expecting her to forbid me to go, but that didn't happen. I made new friends, and we always had a great time. We carpooled and traveled to skating rinks in Philadelphia, Maryland, Delaware, and New Jersey.

If anyone had tried to warn me about going with a wild crowd or getting myself into trouble, I would have laughed out loud. Not me, I was a goody two shoes. Not with this crowd, either. These were my friends. They were all solid young people with jobs and good families. There was no reason for concern.

One particular Saturday night stands out in my memory. A group of us met at our rink in Chester, Pennsylvania. We decided to go to a rink in South Philadelphia just for the fun of it. We were curious to see if our rink was the best, like we believed it was. Six of us piled into one big car and immediately the chatter and laughter began. It seemed like we spent all night laughing. Everything anyone said was funny. We were just a bunch of young people out for an evening of fun. This was going to be a great night.

Off we went into the night. The couple we went with was older. Both were at least twenty-one years of age. My goodness, they were adults; old enough to be our chaperones. They were even engaged.

The rink in South Philly was nice but not as good as ours. The hours flew by. I met a bunch of people and had a great time. Finally, it was time to head home to the suburbs. A lively discussion arose regarding who was going to ride with whom. We had picked up several extra people who needed rides home. A set of seventeen-year-old twins hitched a ride with us. They were only going to West Philly, so it wasn't a problem. It wasn't all that far. As we were about to leave, one of the guys in our group yelled to our driver, "Hey, don't let those twins ride in the same car. They are trouble. You will regret it." The twins laughed and so did we. Our driver simply shrugged his shoulders and told the twins to go ahead and get in the car.

Amid much chatter and laughter, we made our way through the narrow city streets until we came to an industrial area. A wide street named Island Road would take us to the twins' neighborhood. The problem was, there was a roadblock at the entrance to Island Road. Our driver slowed way down and simply drove around the roadblock amid great gales of laughter. Only a short way down the street, one of the twins held up a burning gas lantern that had been on the road block.

"Look what I got!" he hollered.

Quickly, our driver pulled the car to the side of the road and a brief scuffle ensued. He extinguished the flame and stowed the lantern under the seat for safe keeping. Again, this was followed by much laughter.

Continuing on our way, several people pointed out how deserted the area was. There were no buildings or businesses; it was mostly flat dirt. But, the rats; oh boy, did the rats run when the headlights shone on them. With great encouragement from everyone in the car, our driver proceeded to try to hit the rats as they darted across the road in front of us. The car zigzagged from one side of the road to the other and we all thought this was great fun. I don't remember actually running over any of the rats. They were really fast and many of them were huge! They were ugly, too.

We came to a neighborhood of row houses that was home to one of our passengers. The car stopped at the curb to let him off. Someone remarked that it must be time for garbage pickup the next morning and commented on those "tiny little garbage cans out by the curb." I'd never seen a garbage can so small. They weren't any more than twelve to fifteen inches tall. There was one in front of every house. We decided that it must be a "city" thing.

The car pulled away from the curb and continued on down the narrow city street. We'd turned a couple of corners and were well out of the neighborhood when the second twin suddenly held up one of those little, tiny garbage cans, lifted the lid, and yelled, "Look what I got!"

Again, amid much laughter and hooting and hollering, someone managed to get the lid back on the can.

"You have to take that back where you got it," our driver said.

"I can't remember!" the twin said.

Laughter exploded again.

Our driver pulled to the curb and someone set the garbage pail out on the curb and we drove off. The thing I couldn't figure out was how those twins managed to get the lantern and the garbage pail in the car without anyone seeing them.

We arrived at the twins' house and dropped them off. Immediately, the noise level and hysteria in the car calmed down. We drove back to the rink in Chester where most of us had parked our cars. It was well after 1:00 a.m. when we arrived. Still laughing and joking about what a great evening it had been, we said goodnight and I headed home. I smiled all the way home, thinking about all the fun we'd had. I couldn't remember a time when I had enjoyed myself so much. I went to bed with a smile on my face. Of course, I never said a word to my foster mother about where we'd gone or what time I got home. In fact, I don't believe I ever told anyone about that night; at least, not until years later.

Time went on and I often thought about that night. Somehow, that particular group of us never found an opportunity to get together again. The driver (I can't even remember his name) and his date got married and moved on. We all went our separate ways.

Several years passed before I began to realize just what had happened that night. You might say that I needed to grow up. Somewhere I had heard that the twins each had a juvenile record. I didn't believe that. They were just a couple of fun characters. As I learned more about driving and the laws that were in existence at the time, my eyes were opened, and I was shocked at our behavior.

If we'd been stopped by the police, I figured they could have brought a long list of charges against us. *But, I didn't do anything wrong! I was simply a passenger. I was just along for the ride.* Can you just imagine my trying to explain that to a police officer?

Once I sorted it out in my mind, I was appalled. The list of laws we broke would probably have started with joyriding. Yes, stuffing ten people in a car made for six and driving wildly down a street trying to hit rats would have definitely qualified as "joyriding." You could be arrested for that. Then, of course, there was speeding and drag racing (yes, we'd managed to get a bit of that in, too). Although the driver and his date were over eighteen, the rest of us were not. Let's see, breaking curfew. I believe curfew for those under eighteen was 11:00 p.m. at that time. How about contributing to the delinquency of a minor? If the twins really had juvenile records, we were encouraging their lawless trend. Oh, and then there was the theft of public property (the lantern) and the theft of private property (the garbage can). I never had any intention of doing anything wrong that night. I just wanted to go roller skating with my friends, but things escalated quickly.

Chapter 24
Signposts

There is a place in my imagination where I go and look back on the road that my life has taken. Many twists, turns, and curves exist, and through all of them, I see one consistent thing—"signposts" all along my way. Oh, these are not actual signs made of metal or wood but rather people whom I firmly believe God placed in my life at strategic moments when I most needed their guidance.

Our neighborhood was a community, not just a collection of houses and neighbors. These were people who knew each other and cared about one another. As kids, we knew we were safe in that neighborhood. We knew we could trust everyone on that street. If we needed help, we could go to any one of these folks and they would have provided it. We were also well aware that if we got in trouble at a neighbor's house, our parents would be informed immediately!

Everything I needed was just a short walk from my house. The park where we celebrated the 4th of July every year was just six houses up the street. Facing that park, was Norwood Elementary School, where I spent my first six years of school. The Acme grocery store was just a little farther than my school. It was on the corner of Winona Avenue and Chester Pike. The

"Pike" was the main artery to the world outside of our little borough. McManus' Candy Store was between the school and The Acme. We had a deep assurance of security in that community.

The first of these living signposts I remember is little Mrs. Gilcrest who lived four houses up the street. She always had a smile and a friendly greeting for me. Most of the adults in my life simply told me what to do. "Clean up your room." "Go to bed." "Do Your Homework." Mrs. Gilcrest treated me like a real person. She was like a loving aunt who really cared about me. When I saw her working in her yard, I'd go over to say hello. We talked about everything. She wanted to know how I was doing in school. She showed me her garden and explained how she took care of the different plants. Mrs. Gilcrest was my friend. I might have been her favorite among the neighborhood kids. At least I liked to think I was. Perhaps she was just that warm and welcoming to everyone she knew, but I remember feeling so special when she spent time with me.

Mrs. Hipple was a gentle lady with a ready smile, while Frankie, who lived next door to her, had a rather big voice for a lady. I used to wonder how she got the name Frankie, although, I never thought to ask. Frankie was supposed to be a man's name, wasn't it? She was always "Aunt Frankie" to us kids.

The Brightons lived across the street. Their house faced ours. Mr. and Mrs. Brighton owned a variety store on Chester Pike. They were friendly and good neighbors. Their daughter, Carol Lee, and I spent a lot of time playing together. Hopscotch was one of our favorite games. She and I often teased one another about the similarities of our names.

The Rappolds lived two houses up from the Brightons. Their son, Kurt, was shy and I remember how easily he blushed. We teased him just to get him to turn red in the face. Kurt was always doing chores around the house. His dad had him on a pretty tight schedule as I recall. I learned a work ethic from watching this family. The kids in the neighborhood often talked about Kurt cutting the grass and doing other chores while we were all playing. We talked about how Mr. Rappold made Kurt do a lot of chores. However, Kurt's dad was always out there working right alongside him. The neighborhood kids had much respect for this family and Kurt grew up to be a fine man of integrity.

The Ackroyds lived next door to us. This was another family who modeled integrity. I saw Mr. Ackroyd go to work day after day, year in and year out. He worked at a bank. Mrs. Ackroyd was the kind of mom I could only dream of having. Their son, Robert, and I sat out on our back steps many a summer night and just talked. He goes by "Bob" today and we are still friends.

Mrs. Ackroyd was much younger than my foster mother. I remember a conversation I overheard between them. Mrs. Ackroyd was very concerned that her daughter was two years old and was not talking yet. Bessie simply told her not to worry. She went on to say that when Doris was ready to talk, she would and then there would be times that they would wish she'd hush. Sometime later, I overheard another conversation in which Mrs. Ackroyd was acknowledging just how right my foster mother had been.

Mrs. Smith was my first-grade teacher. She introduced me to the joy of reading. Mrs. Smith didn't raise her voice or criticize. She was firm and yet affirming. She smiled and made me feel welcome in her classroom. I adored her. I had not had much experience with really nice people. She showed me how letters made words and words made sentences. Then, sentences made wonderful stories. Mrs. Smith opened a whole new world for me.

Mrs. Hicks was my third-grade teacher. She was soft-spoken and rather shy. She was a proper lady; I could readily see that. Like Mrs. Smith, she let me know I was welcome in her class and she applauded my every success.

One beautiful spring day, Mrs. Hicks took us all to the school auditorium to listen to a radio broadcast of *Peter and the Wolf.* There was an atmosphere of quiet excitement as we took our seats. I've always been a sucker for a great story and this one was just that. In the introduction, we were told that different musical instruments would play the voices of the characters in the drama. As the story unfolded, I sat still and quiet. I don't think I moved through the entire broadcast. I was disappointed when it ended. To this day, I love to hear the early recordings of that story. It has become a classic. I will always associate Mrs. Hicks with the production of *Peter and the Wolf.* She and I shared that one thing—the love of a good story.

Mary Ann Coggin was my third-grade Sunday school teacher at Norwood Methodist Church. She was the first person to help me really understand Who God is. My concept of God initially came from Bessie who had told me He was a God of judgment and punishes those who do wrong. Mary Ann, on the other hand, told me Bible stories I'd never heard; stories of God's love and care for His people. She planted a seed in my heart and introduced me to a God who was much different from my foster mother's depiction. This God was loving and caring.

I will never forget the dear lady in Darby who gave me a whole dollar and then watched to make sure I was safe going down the hill to the trolley. I know that the Lord must have blessed her richly.

Those early years were so difficult and confusing. At home, I couldn't do anything right. I was never able to measure up to my foster mother's expectations and derogatory comments. However, at school or playing with friends, the messages I received were different. I could succeed and I did have something to offer. I had friends who knew nothing of my problems at home and simply accepted me. I am so blessed because, in the end, the positive messages found their way into my heart. I refer to all of these neighbors, friends, and teachers as my "signposts."

In one way or another, they all directed me or helped me along the way.

I am not saying that I didn't carry a tremendous amount of pain and hurt that followed me right on through to adulthood. However, the end result has been more positive than negative. I believe I have all my "signposts" to thank for that. I am also certain that I have my God to thank for all of those signposts. He had His hand on my life all through those difficult years. Today, I firmly believe that God is good and life is wonderful.

Chapter 25
Young Love

When I think back to how Harry and I met, I have to laugh. It almost reads like a script for one of those teenage rock and roll movies that were so popular in the 1950s.

Roller dance skating fascinated me. It was very much like ice dancing. Many of the moves were similar. I loved watching the competitions held at our roller rink. As the couples glided around the floor, it reminded me of the movies I'd seen where grandly dressed couples swirled gracefully around the dance floor. I wished I could be one of those dancers.

Judy, one of my friends at the roller rink, was vivacious and fun to be around. Her boyfriend was serving with the Marine Corps in Korea during the waning months of the Korean Conflict. She talked about him often and eventually revealed that they were engaged. His name was Harry. She didn't have a ring and when asked about it, she'd say they'd decided to wait until he came home to make it official. There was no reason for any of us to doubt her word, except that she did have a skating partner. She and her partner were really deeply involved in dance skating competition. They were quite good. They took part in local competitions and often placed at or near the top.

Judy and her partner spent a lot of time together. They were at the rink most evenings and practiced really hard. However, it was rather obvious they were more than just skating partners. We made sarcastic comments about their relationship. I have to admit, they were often the main topic of our gossip. The joke was that Harry had a big surprise coming when he got home from Korea. Although we never said anything to Judy, we were not always kind when we talked about them among ourselves.

One evening, Judy's thirteen-year-old sister skated up to me with a flourish and said, "Guess who's here?"

"Who?" I said.

"Harry."

"Harry, who?"

She laughed. "You know, Harry, the Marine. He's home from Korea."

"Oh." I wasn't really interested. After all, he wasn't my boyfriend.

Later in the evening, Judy introduced me to Harry. He seemed nice and I was glad he'd made it home safely from Korea. Harry and I talked a bit and I was surprised when he asked me if I wanted to skate a couples dance with him. I had no idea what might be going on between Judy and him, but he acted like he was just having a good time, so I agreed.

Harry and I skated most of the couples skates for the rest of the evening. When the rink was closing, he asked me if he could take me home.

Well, Miss Independent promptly said, "I have my own car."

So he asked if he could pick me up the next night.

I was puzzled, wondering what had happened to Judy, but I didn't ask questions. I simply said, "Okay."

When Harry asked for directions to my house, I tried to explain how to get there. My sense of direction is notoriously bad. By the time I'd finished giving him directions, I had him completely confused.

He finally laughed and shook his head. "How about if I just follow you home tonight?"

I figured that was the simplest solution, so off we went.

Harry drove a 1948 Chevrolet Coupe. My car was a 1952 Chevrolet Sport Coupe. I don't remember who laid down the challenge, but suddenly there we were, drag racing from one traffic light to the next. I was doing pretty well, holding my own until we crossed into Ridley Park. If you didn't live in the suburban Philadelphia area, you probably would not have been aware when you left one town or borough and entered the next. Those of us who lived there were familiar with the boundaries.

As we crossed into the town of Ridley Park, I deliberately let off the gas pedal. I had an excellent reason for that. Just three weeks before, my foster brother, Ed, received a speeding ticket in Ridley Park. That ticket cost him $40.00. Remember, this was the 1950s. That was a lot of money to me. I even knew the daughter of Ridley Park's chief of police (slightly) and that would have counted for exactly zero. Remember, I was just beginning to have some control over my own life. I was working, making a decent salary, and driving my own car. I was not planning on donating any money to the Ridley Park Police Department. To this day, Harry claims victory. I keep telling him, "I could have taken you anytime I wanted."

Chapter 26
Free at Last

Harry and I began seeing each other every night. Skating occupied six nights a week and we were in church on the seventh night. We just fit together. I didn't ask a lot of questions, but he did tell me that he and Judy had ended their relationship.

Three weeks after the drag race, I was sure Harry was the man I would marry. I am certain God showed me clearly that this was His will for both of us.

As usual, things were not going to be easy from here on. Bessie never approved of anyone I dated. This time was no exception. The day after she met Harry, she lectured me for a long time, criticizing everything about him. She gave me a long laundry list of all his faults. I was so angry! How could she criticize him like that when she knew nothing about him? This time, I decided, she would not ruin everything.

Harry and I spent every possible moment together. The subject of marriage came up rather soon but we agreed that we would wait until we could win my foster mother's approval. We were way too optimistic.

I'd been dating Harry for almost eleven months when things suddenly turned ugly. One Saturday, we had plans to go out as usual. My foster mother always insisted that I let her know where I was going, who I would be with, and what time we'd be home. Actually, she dictated the time we were to be home. This particular night, there were big doings. First, a friend was getting married. We wanted to attend the wedding and the reception. After that, we planned to go to a movie at the Chester Pike Drive-In. The joke in our area was, if a movie played the Chester Pike Drive-In, that would be its last showing and it would never be seen again.

I took great pains to talk with Bessie several times during the week. Over and over, I reminded her of our plans and that we would be late in coming home. I made sure she had the time of the wedding and the reception and I explained that the movie would end late. I reminded her again on Saturday.

Harry and I arrived back at my house at about 1:30 a.m.

Bessie was standing with her hands on her hips waiting for us. "Where in the hell have you been?"

I tried hard to answer civilly. I could feel hot, blazing anger rising up inside. I was so frustrated. "I told you that we had a big evening planned and that we would be late. I've reminded you about it all week long."

Bessie shouted. "You never told me any such thing! What do you mean by coming home at this ridiculous hour?"

Harry was not intimidated by this lady at all. He spoke up quickly. "I think she's old enough to decide for herself what time she comes home." That lit the fire and Bessie turned her anger on him. I told him he'd better leave. He argued that he was concerned about leaving me alone with this angry woman. He was worried about what might happen. I pushed him out the door and assured him I'd be all right. He left, very reluctantly.

When Harry was gone, Bessie turned her full fury on me. She went over and over the points of her lecture. "It's your health I'm concerned about." Then she tried to say it was my reputation that worried her. She said if I didn't care about it, she did. I tried hard to be reasonable, but she would have none of that. We sat in the living room until 5:30 in the morning. All the while she lectured. She said the same things over and over again.

Suddenly, she threw her up her hands and her tone grew cold. "I think you'd better go live with your mother!"

I tried to protest. I told her I didn't believe she really meant that. While I was saying it, I knew in my heart that this was exactly what I wanted. I also knew it would do no good to try reasoning with her because her mind was made up.

She turned on her heel and stormed up the stairs to her bedroom. I would not have said it to her, but I was secretly relieved and excited. I was eighteen and had aged out of the foster-care system. Bessie no longer received any money for my care from the state. I believed that was really the motivating factor in her decision.

I sat alone in the living room for a long time. I knew I could not call my mother at 5:30 a.m., even though I was so excited that I could hardly wait. Finally, around 7:00 a.m., I knew my mother would be up and I decided it was a good time to call. When she answered the phone, I simply said, "I'm being evicted."

"Well, pack your things and come on."

My life as a foster kid was over!

Chapter 27
God Is Faithful

In a hurry to begin my new life, I packed only what I thought I really needed, leaving childhood treasures behind. I didn't care what happened to them. I was certain Bessie would just throw them all away. Sadly, in later years, I wished I had those Storybook Dolls and all my books. I would have enjoyed passing them on to my own children. However, at that moment, I was not thinking of children or grandchildren. My only concern was getting out of that house. Freedom was mine! I never saw Bessie again.

A curtain dropped, ending this phase of my life. Immediately, another lifted, introducing the next act. My job, church, and boyfriend were all in the suburbs. My home was now in Philadelphia with my mother and brother. There was no time to prepare. I simply began living my new life. The commute to work was different. It took longer and there was more traffic.

Many nights I arrived home just in time to fall into bed so I could get up and go to work the next day. However, there was a big difference. I was no longer greeted with angry, hurtful words. I didn't have to be on guard for confrontation. Mother and Bill were glad to see me. We shared easy laughter. We became a family again. For the first time in fourteen years, I felt I was home.

It didn't take long for me to realize that this arrangement was not ideal. Mother was glad we were all together, yet I could see how inconvenient it was for her. She hadn't shared a bedroom for many years and never one with a teenager. The apartment was small, having only two bedrooms, and one bath. Traveling between the city and the suburbs was time-consuming, expensive, and tiring. Harry and I talked more seriously about our marriage. My foster mother had been our only reason for waiting and she was no longer in the picture. We began to make our plans.

Life became very exciting. We were planning our wedding. It would have to be a small wedding because we didn't have a lot of money. We arranged for the church and asked our pastor, Dan, to perform the ceremony. I asked my best friend, Bev, to be my bridesmaid. Harry asked his friend, Bud, to be best man. We chose September 21 as our wedding day. I was still trying to get used to making my own decisions. Sometimes, I felt totally overwhelmed.

Mother wanted to buy my wedding dress, so we made plans to go shopping. We found a lovely dress. It was coral and fit very well. Coral has always been a good color for me. However, there was a problem. I really wanted a white wedding dress. I worried about how to tell my mother, afraid I would hurt her feelings. We were, after all, only in the beginning stages of this new phase of our mother/daughter relationship. I worried and fretted for weeks. I kept forgetting that I could make my own decisions. I was afraid mother would be angry if I said I didn't want to wear the coral dress.

Our wedding date was coming closer and closer. Time was running out for me to change my mind about the dress. One afternoon, I decided to wander through a department store near work. As I was leaving the ladies department, I noticed a mannequin wearing the perfect dress. It had white lace, with three-quarter length sleeves. It had a scoop neck and was calf length; very simple and elegant. This was my dress. I found the nearest phone and called Mother. Excitedly, I told her all about the dress.

"If that's what you want, go ahead and buy it." She had no problem with my changing my mind. She even paid for the second dress and I got to keep the coral one, too.

On September 21, 1957, Harry and I became husband and wife. Just eleven people attended, including us and Pastor Dan who'd led me to Christ.

We took up residence in a little third-floor apartment with steep roof gables. We called it, "Early Attic." We couldn't put furniture up against several walls because of the pitch of the roof, but we didn't care. We belonged to each other and life was good. I was amazed at the change my life had taken. In a few short months, I'd transitioned from a life of fear, stress, anger, and tension to what I called a "normal" life. I was a married woman, loved and respected by my husband.

Several years went by. I was a young wife with a wonderful husband and two beautiful children, a boy and a girl. We had a little house in Chester, Pennsylvania that wasn't much, but it was ours.

One Spring day, the children were upstairs taking their naps, so I took advantage of the extra time to catch up on some cleaning chores. While running the vacuum in the living room,

I was thinking about how blessed and different my life was now compared to my growing up years. Suddenly, a thought hit me like a shock. I stopped in the middle of that room. Speaking aloud to my Father, I said, "Lord, You have done exactly what You promised me so many years ago. You, Lord Jesus, have taken my upside-down life and turned it right-side-up."

Epilogue

When the Lord laid on my heart that I should write my story, I resisted, strongly. Fear was the main reason. Who in the world was I to write a book? Much of the story I didn't want to recall, let alone write for others to read. I had often joked about writing a book someday. I would say, "I'd have to make it a work of fiction, because no one would believe it."

My husband and I started a new job. We were in the process of learning a whole new set of skills. We shared a twelve-hour work day in a new location. I brazenly asked my Father, "Do you see what we're dealing with down here, and you want me to do what?" I pulled what I call a "Scarlett O'Hara. In the movie *Gone with the Wind*, Scarlett is the main character. Anytime she doesn't want to deal with an issue, she simply puts her hand up and says, "I'll think about that tomorrow." That is exactly what I did. Seven years passed, and I often felt guilty about not writing. We found ourselves in a new city working the same job. However, this one was much easier. The hours were like banker's hours compared to the first place. Suddenly, I had an impression of my Father standing with His arms folded, tapping his toe, saying to me, "I'm still waiting." He continued, "Do you realize you have been disobedient to me for seven years?" I stuttered and stammered. "You were serious about that", I asked. I just knew the lightning was going to strike.

I asked the Lord to forgive me and I promised Him that I would try. I had no confidence in my ability. I thought I'd put everything behind me. I learned very quickly that I'd not put it behind me at all. I had simply stuffed it down deep inside. When I began to write, I was surprised. I could not get it down on the page fast enough. The story poured out of my heart.

However, the process was not easy. At times I was overwhelmed, and I simply quit and put it away; sometimes for months at a time. I could not face it. The whole project took me ten years.

I put off writing about the sexual abuse again and again. Finally, one Thursday night, I felt the Lord saying, "We have an appointment this coming Sunday night." Sunday night was my writing night. I said to the Lord, "I don't want to do this." He said, "I know." That was all. Sunday night came. I sat down at the computer. Once again, the words spilled onto the page.

When I finally finished the story, I sat back in my chair and bowed my head. I told the Lord, that I had done the best I could. I asked forgiveness for being disobedient and taking so long. I thanked him for walking this long path with me.

Around that time, I attended a Bible study in which the teacher talked about a whole new concept I'd never heard. She said that when we are obedient to God, he gives us blessings as a result. She also said that many times He gives us extra blessings. She called them special gifts.

For three days after I finished writing, I was exhausted. I didn't want to do anything. Then I realized I was beginning to feel differently. I slowly came to understand that the Lord had worked three wonderful miracles. First, I have complete peace for the first time in my life. Second, the scars in my heart are gone; not just healed over but gone. The one issue I struggled with for many years, was forgiveness. When I became a Christian, friends shared with me that I would have to forgive my foster mother and the man who sexually abused me. I was angry and hurt. I could not imagine being able to forgive. For years, I prayed the Lord would forgive them for me, because I could not do it. The third miracle He has given me as a result of obeying Him, is forgiveness. Even though both my foster mother and the man who abused me have passed away, I know that if I could meet them today, I would be able to say to them, "I forgive you." However, that's not the end of it. The real gift of the forgiveness is that I am the one who has been freed from the guilt and the pain. I am finally free.

Made in United States
Orlando, FL
14 May 2023

33150351R00075